WINERIES WITH STYLE

Peter Richards

WINERIES WITH STYLE

MITCHELL BEAZLEY

Almaviva CHILE

For my family

Wineries with Style
by Peter Richards

First published in Great Britain in 2004 by Mitchell Beazley, an imprint of Octopus Publishing Group Limited, 2–4 Heron Quays, London E14 4JP.

Copyright © Octopus Publishing Group Ltd 2004
Text © Peter Richards 2004
Maps © Octopus Publishing Group Ltd 2004

All rights reserved. No part of this publication may be reproduced or used in any form by any means, electronic or mechanical, including photocopying, recording or by any information storage or retrieval system, without the prior written permission of the publishers.

A CIP catalogue record for this book is available from the British Library.

ISBN 1840009004

The author and publishers will be grateful for any information that will assist them in keeping future editions up-to-date. Although all reasonable care has been taken in the preparation of this book, neither the publishers, editors nor the author can accept any liability for any consequences arising from the use thereof, or the information contained therein.

Commissioning Editor: Hilary Lumsden
Executive Art Editor: Yasia Williams
Managing Editor: Juanne Branquinho
Editor: Susan Low
Design: Tim Pattinson
Map: Kenny Grant / Tim Pattinson
Production: Gary Hayes

Typeset in Giovanni and Aurea
Printed and bound in China

Cos d'Estournel FRANCE

CONTENTS

Introduction	8
Wineries Around the World	10

The Icon Approach 14
Great Estates
Château Margaux FRANCE Villa di Maser ITALY
Château Ksara LEBANON Castel Noarna ITALY
Schloss Vollrads GERMANY Schloss Johannisberg
GERMANY Abbazia di Novacella ITALY Mönchhof
GERMANY FWW AUSTRIA Staatlicher Hofkeller Würzburg
GERMANY Massandra UKRAINE Cos d'Estournel FRANCE

In Brief 38

Sounds of The Underground 40
The Labyrinthine World of the Wine Cellar
Domecq La Mezquita SPAIN Pommery FRANCE
Terra-Vinéa FRANCE Château Ausone FRANCE
Redi ITALY Mastroberardino ITALY González-Byass SPAIN
Château Lafite-Rothschild FRANCE Raimat SPAIN
Codorníu SPAIN Artesa USA Juan Alcorta SPAIN
Salentein ARGENTINA Jarvis USA

In Brief 66

Graham Beck Coastal Cellar SOUTH AFRICA

A Breath of Fresh Air 68
Breathing New Life into Traditional Surroundings
Clos Pegase USA Château Pichon-Longueville Baron FRANCE Château d'Arsac FRANCE Hess Collection USA Chivite Señorío de Arínzano SPAIN Badia a Coltibuono ITALY Loimer AUSTRIA Schloss Wackerbarth GERMANY López de Heredia SPAIN Hermann J. Wiemer USA Rustenberg SOUTH AFRICA Tahbilk AUSTRALIA Mitchelton AUSTRALIA Te Mata NEW ZEALAND

In Brief 96

Ancient Made Modern 98
The Past Gets a Modern Makeover
Alois Lageder Löwengang ITALY Summerhill CANADA Romanin FRANCE Domaine Viret Clos du Paradis FRANCE Séptima ARGENTINA Ca' Marcanda ITALY Waterford SOUTH AFRICA Mission Hill CANADA Opus One USA Catena Zapata ARGENTINA Sterling USA Boutari Santorini GREECE Shadowfax AUSTRALIA Gracia CHILE

In Brief 128

Immaculate Conceptions 130
Wineries That Lay Winemaking Bare
Viña Real SPAIN Louis Jadot La Sablière FRANCE Craggy Range NEW ZEALAND Terre da Vino ITALY Ransom NEW ZEALAND Château Haut Selve FRANCE Dornier SOUTH AFRICA Staatsweingut Weinsberg GERMANY Graham Beck Coastal Cellar SOUTH AFRICA Rymill AUSTRALIA Sileni NEW ZEALAND Santo Tomás MEXICO Malivoire CANADA Haras de Pirque CHILE

In Brief 160

A New World 162
A Stylish Future for Wine
Ysios SPAIN Marqués de Riscal SPAIN Le Clos Jordanne CANADA Irius SPAIN Antion SPAIN Darien SPAIN Dominus USA Disznókő HUNGARY Vergelegen SOUTH AFRICA Mezzacorona ITALY Almaviva CHILE Pérez Cruz CHILE

In Brief 188

Index & Bibliography 190

Note to reader:
in the picture captions ≫ indicates the page number(s) where the principal text for that particular winery is found.

Introduction

It all began in Chile. I was a young journalist working overseas in my first job. I didn't have much free time, but when I did, I drove out of the city to explore. I saw the ocean. Mountains. Weathered faces on bikes, on foot, peering from the back of trucks, crammed into thundering buses. Cake sellers, their baskets stuffed with delicacies, flourished white handkerchiefs at passing vehicles. Endless roadside fruit-and-vegetable stalls touted finest *chirimoya* and *choclo*, the evocative names scribbled clumsily on cardboard signs. Mostly, though, I was intrigued by the vineyards that lined Chile's roads like constant companions. I didn't know much about wine; I liked drinking it, but was wary of what seemed an intimidating subject. Nonetheless, I knew that the vineyards led to wineries and, in the end, I couldn't resist. Once at the winery, my fears seemed to fade away. This was how wine should be enjoyed, I thought, in surroundings that brought the whole thing to life. It gave every wine a story I could relate to. I was hooked.

In a sense, this book began back then. Writing and wine became my full-time profession not long afterwards, but those first experiences remain fresh in my mind. Wine can be a tremendously rich, rewarding experience, but it can also be a daunting subject. It needs to be brought to life. Taking a closer look at the wineries, I believe, is one way to do that. It's a glimpse behind the scenes; a remarkable fusion of wine and architecture; an open invitation to travel and experience this vibrant world for yourself. Above all, it's one integral part of the wine story that has yet to be told.

During my travels to research this book, I lost count of the number of raised eyebrows and mystified expressions that met me when I explained that wine buildings were my focus just as much as wine. One of Burgundy's finest winemakers had to hear it from my own mouth to believe I was for real. Surely wine is all about the vineyards, I could hear them thinking, perhaps even the winemaker – but the wineries?

I hope I can answer such questions with this book. It has been a privilege and pleasure to write, perhaps all the more so for being a fresh take on an otherwise well-documented subject. I've loved every minute of it and am hugely thankful for the opportunity. Drinking great wine is an experience infused with a thrilling sense of history and geography; great winery architecture translates that into visual form.

This book features eighty wineries chosen for their architectural interest. These are wineries that have their own style, that tell a story and put wine on a platform that everyone can reach and enjoy. With just one exception they are all open to visits, though some require advance notice and a few are yet to be built.

It is an entirely personal selection, albeit assembled after much discussion, travel, and research. The humbling aspect of putting a book like this together comes with the realization that there are so many wineries worthy of inclusion. For every wine region around the world there is a gem of a wine estate, often a hidden one; everyone I talked to knew of a favourite or intriguing winery. I can only sympathize with those that have not made the cut and encourage anyone who believes I have been remiss in my selection to get in touch. One of wine's best qualities is that it sparks debate and this book should be no exception.

As far as the book's structure is concerned, I wanted to do something different. Instead of the usual country-by-country approach that most wine books are obliged to adopt, I have split the book into six chapters. Generally speaking, the book moves from old wine estates ("The Icon Approach") to new wineries ("A New World"). The intention was to break down the traditional divisions associated with wine and allow a freer, more global approach. Every winery also has a factbox, that includes wine tips and other quick-reference information. I have not gone into the technical details of how wine is made; there are many other books for that purpose. Also, the map on pages 10–11 is intended simply to put the wineries into their broad geographical context.

The wine world is constantly evolving, but it has never evolved at a faster pace than now. Winery architect Jesús Marino Pascual put it well during a sunlit breakfast in Rioja. "We're living through a change of era, in architecture just as in wine," he told me. "Both wines and wineries are reflecting this evolution. It's a magical moment." Rioja is just one wine region that is experiencing a boom in stunning wineries and there are others. These are exciting times.

The aim of this book is to celebrate some of the great names in wine and architecture and explore how the two come together with captivating results. From Château Margaux to Dominus, from Gustave Eiffel to Frank Gehry, it's a compelling story. It is also a statement that wine does not begin and end with grapes and glasses. True enjoyment of wine comes with an open mind and an appreciation of life's finer things: material and immaterial, elemental and architectural.

However, this is not just a celebration. It's also an appeal against the imitative and uninspiring mind-set that afflicts the wine industry, both in vinous and architectural terms. Many still lack the courage to express and enjoy the character of the land with humility and passion. There's nothing more pitiful than such lack of ambition.

The wine world must celebrate the local, but banish the parochial. As interested consumers, we should support this endeavour and encourage others to follow. What's more, you can have fun while you're doing it, simply by drinking good wine and taking an interest. If this book helps just one person in that endeavour, it will have served its purpose. Above all, I hope wine and its architecture can enrich other lives as it has mine.

The Burgundian winemaker who couldn't quite believe I was for real soon warmed to my cause. In the calm of her cellar we enjoyed a glass of wine together. It was the kind of wine that defies description: tantalizing and teasing the senses, maddeningly brilliant. It was at that moment she expressed my argument far more eloquently than I could have hoped. "Wine is good because it gives you a sense of place," she mused, swirling the wine meditatively in her glass. "Wine cellars exist in a realm beyond time, where we disconnect ourselves from daily concerns. Only then do people open up to themselves and others, indulge in magnificent communication. That is why these are sacred spaces."

Clos Pégase USA

Diznókő HUNGARY

Pérez Cruz CHILE

INTRODUCTION 9

Wineries around the World

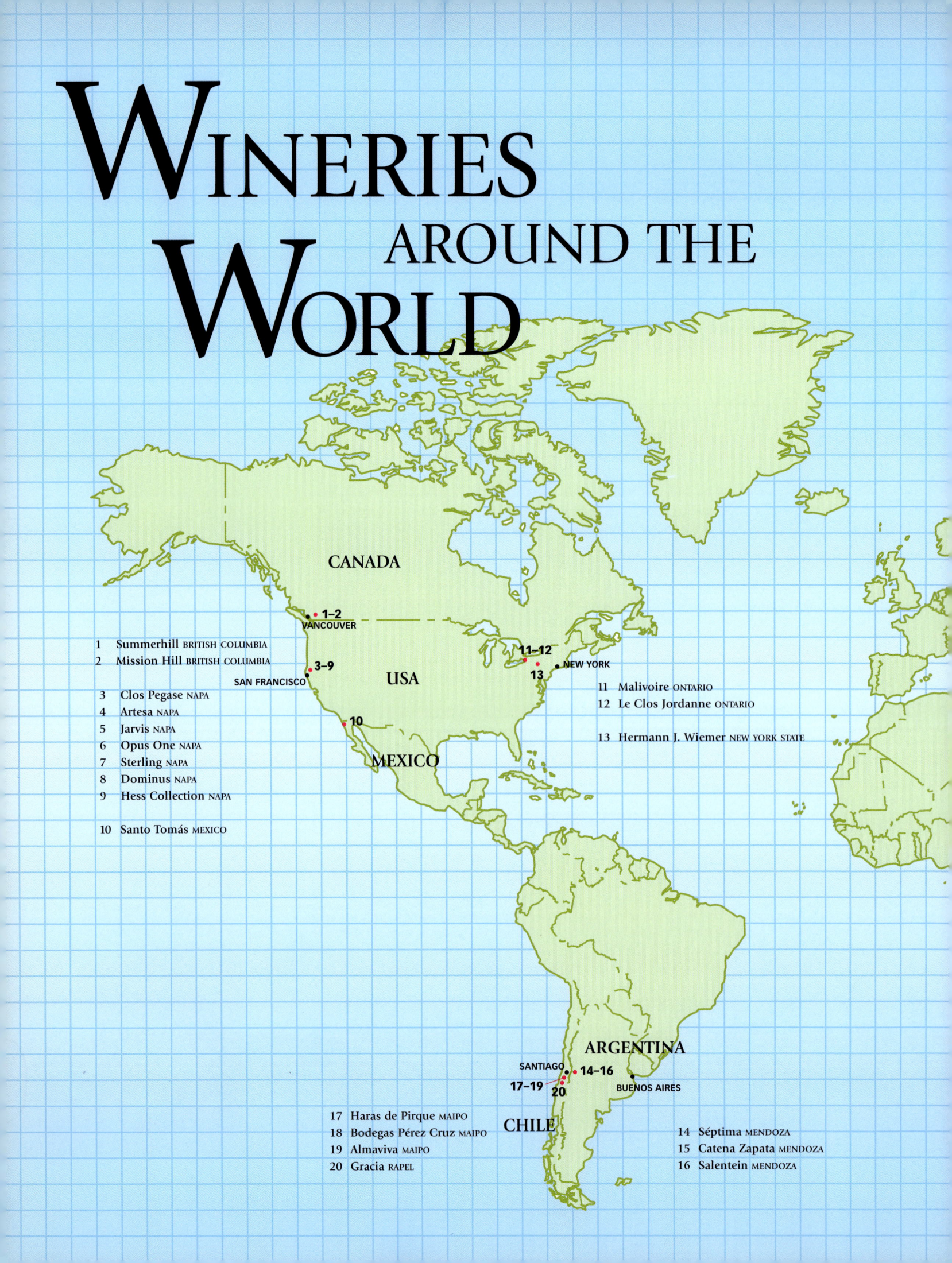

1. Summerhill BRITISH COLUMBIA
2. Mission Hill BRITISH COLUMBIA

3. Clos Pegase NAPA
4. Artesa NAPA
5. Jarvis NAPA
6. Opus One NAPA
7. Sterling NAPA
8. Dominus NAPA
9. Hess Collection NAPA

10. Santo Tomás MEXICO

11. Malivoire ONTARIO
12. Le Clos Jordanne ONTARIO

13. Hermann J. Wiemer NEW YORK STATE

17. Haras de Pirque MAIPO
18. Bodegas Pérez Cruz MAIPO
19. Almaviva MAIPO
20. Gracia RAPEL

14. Séptima MENDOZA
15. Catena Zapata MENDOZA
16. Salentein MENDOZA

☐ **GERMANY**
☐ 34 Schloss Wackerbarth SACHSEN
☐ 35 Schloss Vollrads RHEINGAU
☐ 36 Schloss Johannisberg RHEINGAU
☐ 37 Mönchhof MOSEL-SAAR-RUWER
☐ 38 Staatlicher Hofkeller Würzburg FRANKEN
☐ 39 Staatsweingut Weinsberg WURTTEMBERG

☐ **FRANCE**
☐ 40 Pommery CHAMPAGNE
☐ 41 Louis Jadot BURGUNDY
☐ 42 Margaux BORDEAUX
☐ 43 Lafite Rothschild BORDEAUX
☐ 44 Cos d'Estournel BORDEAUX
☐ 45 d'Arsac BORDEAUX
☐ 46 Pichon-Longueville Baron BORDEAUX
☐ 47 Ausone BORDEAUX
☐ 48 Haute Selve BORDEAUX
☐ 49 Terra-Vinéa LANGUEDOC

☐ 50 Romanin PROVENCE
☐ 51 Domaine Viret Clos du Paradis RHONE

☐ **SPAIN**
☐ 52 Chivite Arínzano NAVARRA
☐ 53 Irius SOMONTANO
☐ 54 Raimat COSTERS DEL SEGRE
☐ 55 Codorníu PENEDÈS
☐ 56 Viña Real RIOJA
☐ 57 Marqués de Riscal RIOJA
☐ 58 Darien RIOJA

☐ 59 Ysios RIOJA
☐ 60 Antion RIOJA
☐ 61 Juan Alcorta RIOJA
☐ 62 López de Heredia RIOJA
☐ 63 Domecq La Mezquita JEREZ
☐ 64 González-Byass JEREZ

☐ **ITALY**
☐ 65 Abbazia di Novacella ALTO ADIGE
☐ 66 Lageder Löwengang ALTO ADIGE
☐ 67 Castel Noarna TRENTINO
☐ 68 Mezzacorona TRENTINO

☐ 69 Villa di Maser VENETO
☐ 70 Terre da Vino PIEMONTE
☐ 71 Ca'Marcanda TUSCANY
☐ 72 Redi TUSCANY
☐ 73 Badia a Coltibuono TUSCANY
☐ 74 Mastroberardino CAMPANIA

OTHER COUNTRIES
75 FWW WACHAU
76 Fred Loimer KAMPTAL
77 Disznókő TOKAJ
78 Massandra CRIMEA
79 Boutari SANTORINI
80 Château Ksara BEKAA VALLEY

21 Dornier STELLENBOSCH
22 Waterford STELLENBOSCH
23 Rustenberg STELLENBOSCH
24 Graham Beck Coastal Cellar FRANSCHHOEK
25 Vergelegen STELLENBOSCH

26 Rymill SOUTH AUSTRALIA
27 Tahbilk VICTORIA
28 Mitchelton VICTORIA
29 Shadowfax VICTORIA

30 Ransom AUCKLAND
31 Te Mata HAWKE'S BAY
32 Craggy Range HAWKE'S BAY
33 Sileni Estates HAWKE'S BAY

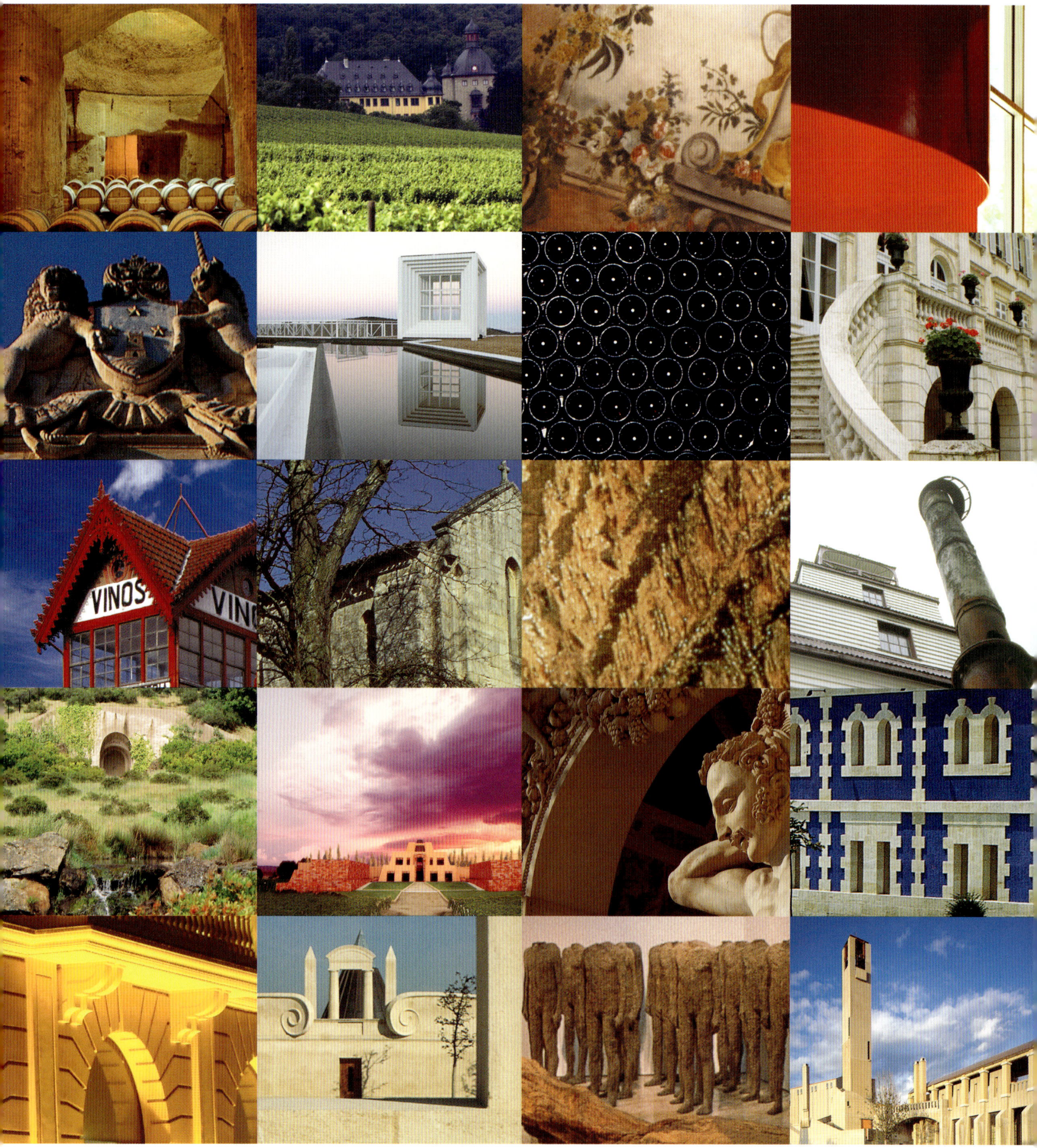
VINOS

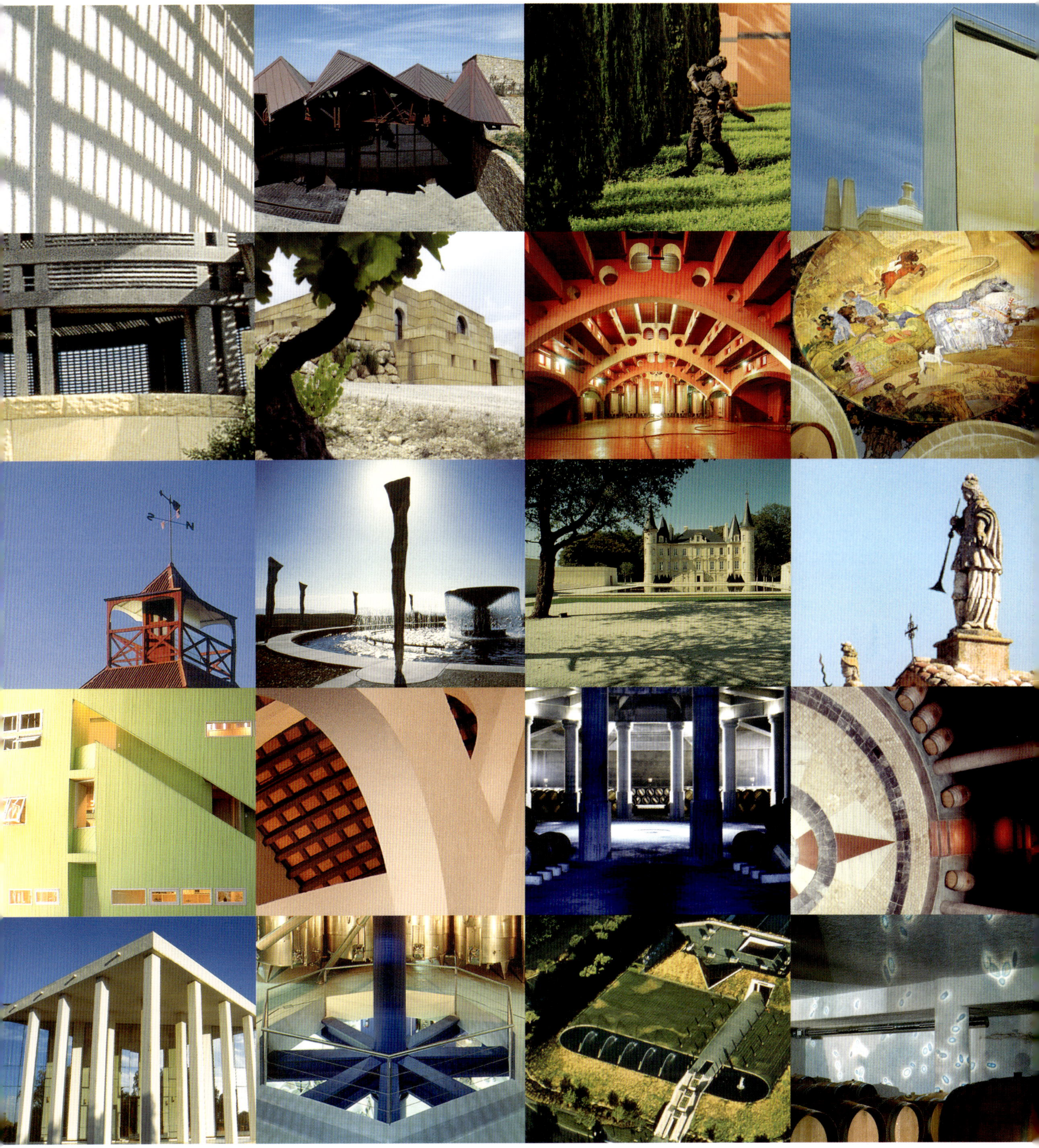

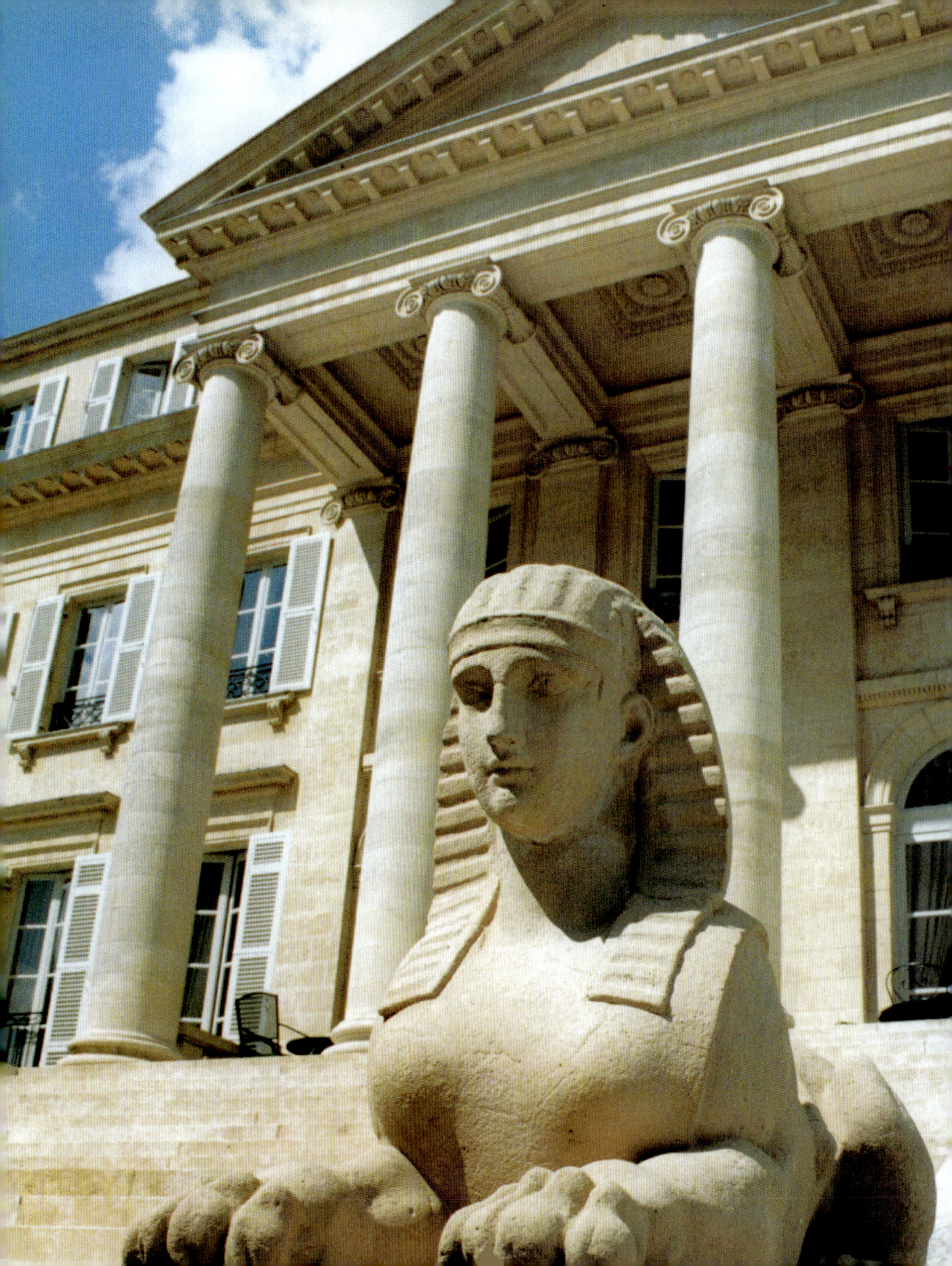

THE ICON APPROACH

GREAT ESTATES

A desire for permanence and beauty is what marks out wine estates as iconic. "In our world, wine becomes tiles, stone, and woodwork," grumbled one wine producer to me about upkeep costs at their magnificent château. It's worth it. Wine has a rich past and these buildings bring it to vivid life.

It is a bright, crisp summer morning on the outskirts of the Black Forest. I am at the delightful Johner winery but it is inspired words, not architecture, that make this visit special. "The grape vine is rooted in the earth, solid. But when you drink its wine you get light, spiritual – like spires on a roof." The words are Irene Johner's; even now they stay fresh in my mind as I write.

"We can sit here, drink wine and forget time," she says, with a nod that takes in the carefully crafted tasting room and its view over rolling vineyards. Neither of us speaks; there's nothing to add. The moment passes only when Irene's husband, winemaker Karl, bustles in, slightly late and endearingly flustered. "What did I miss?" he asks.

Change is inevitable in this world, but some things remain constant. Wine has much the same effect on drinkers today as when it was first consumed millennia ago – an experience Irene Johner describes so evocatively. In those early days, they didn't know why, but somehow this magic grape juice made them feel alive, almost omnipotent – until the headache set in. From those beginnings, the story of wine emerges in the first glimmers of what we now call civilization, when humans were beginning to turn from a nomadic existence to a more sedentary lifestyle. It was around 8000BC, in the fertile plains and vine-friendly uplands in and around the Middle East and Caucasus Mountains.

You can imagine the scene. The drive to cultivate regular crops has rooted man to the spot. Primitive, isolated shelters give way to a more collective, permanent way of life. People eat, drink, and talk together, and life becomes about more than just the mundane. This went beyond mere survival; it was culture.

The emergence of settled human society is marked by more than just the allegiance to the vine; it is also the start of architecture. In *The Story of Architecture*, Jonathan Glancey points out that building is not the same thing as architecture. Animals can build, but architecture implies that there is science and artistry to the endeavour. In the same way, good wine is more than just fermented grapes; it needs a skilled and ambitious hand to manage the process. The raw materials for wine and architecture pre-date humanity, but can be transformed by the human touch into profound and inspirational form. In Irene's words, both wine and architecture invite people to get light and spiritual – to look up and think.

Beauty, usefulness, and permanence – the three essential qualities of architecture, according to the Roman military engineer and architect Vitruvius, author of the earliest extant treatise on the subject. Wine and architecture already had a history at the time of imperial Rome; Vitruvius' words were to prove a classic formula for many years to come in architecture of all spheres, including that of wine.

THE ICON APPROACH 17

18 WINERIES WITH STYLE

Villa di Maser ITALY

THE ICON APPROACH

Castel Noarna ITALY >>24, 27

Château Ksara LEBANON >>24

Castel Noarna ITALY

Take Château Margaux, for example, one of the classic landmarks in wine, located in Bordeaux. Margaux was built in the early nineteenth century by architect Louis Combes. What's great about Margaux is the way it all fits together so well – Combes' self-stated ambition was for simplicity, unity, and aptness, to echo Vitruvius. The iconic image of Margaux is the château, but the impression is so much more: the tree-lined avenue, gardens, estate buildings, and vineyards. This is not a winery in the modern sense, where everything from winemaking to entertaining happens in the same building. It is an example of a traditional wine estate, where the château is the residence, and the winemaking takes place in the *chais* and *cuviers*, practical outbuildings. But, at Margaux it all comes together with such unity and coherence that the experience is hard to describe – peace and permanence are two words that come close.

I watched the sun come up over Margaux. The air was moist and chilly; a slight haze drifted lazily across from the vineyards, softening the château's impeccable bright lines. I was reminded of how Margaux's wine was once memorably described as pure finesse, leaving the breath pure and the mouth cool. Cellarmaster Paul Pontallier talked to me about how such an environment helps him in his daily work. "It's such a privileged place, so coherent, so refined," he says. "It definitely influences the spirit in which we work. It reflects our ambitions for the wine. We're proud of it."

Château Margaux has become something of an icon. This is not simply down to its stunning architecture; it's also the fact that the wine made here is among the finest that money can buy. It's the combination of the two that is such a powerful proposition. Not only are the product and the image in perfect tandem; the whole package acts like an open invitation to experience the rich and vibrant world of wine. Some people criticize Margaux's image as elitist. I call it inspired.

20 WINERIES WITH STYLE

Château Ksara LEBANON

As a classic landmark in wine, Margaux sets a standard. It is one of the many architectural statements in Bordeaux that have helped create a mystique, not just about the region's wines, but also about the very word "château". So much so that people often think of Bordeaux châteaux as the sole trendsetters, the original alliance of wine and architecture. But is this really the case? There are many reasons why not; just one can be found across the Alps, in Italy.

Margaux is often described as Palladian in style and it's a term that deserves explanation. Andrea Palladio was a sixteenth-century stonemason who, after absorbing Vitruvius and the Renaissance spirit, became one of the most influential architects of all time. He advocated measured unity and classical harmony in architecture; such is Margaux. But Palladio's legacy to wine is not limited simply to his influence. The real thing can be found near Venice.

The Villa Barbaro in Maser, or Villa di Maser as it is known today, is a wine estate in the Veneto region of northern Italy. It is an architectural treasure. Built by Palladio in the 1550s for the Barbaro brothers, it was designed as a home, farm estate house, stables, and winery. All things, Palladio wrote in *I Quattro Libri dell Architettura*, "essential for a farm".

I pull up at Maser when the last, deep golden rays of sunshine are slanting across the villa's dramatic façade. Before all that classical splendour I need a bite to eat, though, so I pop into the bar. Chewing on my cheese and ham toasty, I ask the barman about Maser. He sidles up close and looks conspiratorial. "Forget the architecture, try the Merlot," he says in Italian. *"Una bomba."*

As palatable as the wine undoubtedly is, however, it is Maser's architecture that steals the show. The nearby temple, dovecotes with sundials, statues, and Greek-temple façade all create a great sense of occasion. The five-part façade Palladio uses here has become a staple of western architecture – Washington DC's Capitol is one example. This fact is noted by Carl I Gable, who also points to Palladio's twofold genius in not only creating an architectural gem, but also in doing so for comparatively little money. Such methods have inspired architects since.

The biggest struggle for architects is usually with their client and their budget, as Palladio himself grumbles in a rare moment of indulgence. But, he overcomes these hurdles in style. He improvises, using imposing exterior features to draw attention away from penny-saving materials and, inside, where hung tapestries were common, he has frescoes painted instead. One lively number depicts Bacchus crushing grapes into a golden goblet.

It is quite something to hear a voice from the Italian Renaissance speaking about the architecture of wineries. Palladio is, as ever, practical and detailed, describing how winery floors should "be made to slope a little towards the middle," so that if wine were spilled, it could be retrieved. He notes how any light must enter from the north and east, to prevent wine becoming "weak and ruined by being warmed up by the heat".

Nowadays, the winemaking takes place in a mid-nineteenth century winery a stone's throw from the villa. By and large it respects Palladio's specifications concerning overall estate unity. Wandering around the estate, you can just imagine Palladio allowing himself a break to sip wine on the terrace of the newly completed villa with his patrons the Barbaro brothers. He might have been in need of the "great refreshment and consolation", as he wrote, required by "spirits tired of the agitation of the city".

One such agitation weighing on Venetian minds was Columbus' recent discovery of the New World, which threatened Venice's control over Mediterranean trade routes. It was an early sign of what would eventually become the fierce and ultimately fruitful rivalry between Old and New Worlds of wine in the twentieth century.

But the story of the architecture of wine doesn't start with Palladio, either. It stretches back through medieval times into ancient civilizations, when we can only guess at how wine estates looked. We can, however, get a sense of that past if we look at where it all started. Nowhere can claim to epitomize

Schloss Vollrads GERMANY

Schloss Johannisberg GERMANY >>27

the Old World of wine more than the Near and Middle East. It is here that wine is thought to have first been cultivated and consumed on a wide scale. Archaeologists have unearthed evidence suggesting as much in Turkey, Syria, Jordan, and Lebanon dating as far back as 8000BC – the early society we saw at the start of the chapter.

Subsequent civilizations also learned to cherish wine and it crops up in Egyptian tombs, Phoenician shipping history, and Roman writing. Château Ksara, in Lebanon's Bekaa Valley, offers a tantalizing glimpse into that history. It is built on Roman tunnels, now serving as cellars, which are just one of the many signs of Roman influence in the region – another can be found at nearby Baalbek, where spectacular ruins include a monumental temple to Bacchus, god of wine.

Wine's distant past, as it survives today, tends to be largely an underground affair. As we shall see in this chapter and the next, underground places tend to be cool, dark, easily protected, and usually immune from demolition – the perfect location for valuable wine and self-preservation. Buildings, by contrast, have a nasty habit of getting destroyed. Caves and tunnels were probably man's first shelters; when they were vacated, wine could move in.

While Ksara's Roman tunnels aren't necessarily the earliest example of a winery, they are a tantalizing glimpse into wine history. And not only Roman history – Ksara is so named because it was the site of a *ksar*, or fortress, at the time of the Crusades. Religion is never far from wine; indeed, the property as it is now was founded in 1857 by Jesuits; the barrel room, with its spartan mud, cedar, and straw roof, was their refectory or dining room.

Ksara's tunnels were expanded during World War I and now extend nearly two kilometres (one and a quarter miles) underground. In general, however, conflict has rarely helped Ksara and its fellow Lebanese wine-growers – the hot, high Bekaa Valley, famed for producing strapping red wine, is no stranger to bloodshed. Stories of driving trucks of grapes through artillery barrages at harvest time are not unfamiliar.

Nowhere is the concept of conflict enshrined more memorably than in the castle. The word château ultimately derives from the Latin term for castle, *castellum*, even though many wine châteaux look remarkably unlike what we would consider a castle in its strictest sense. But, like the word, castles themselves have evolved over time to suit the requirements of the age. Castel Noarna is closer to the typical idea of a castle and is in fact a rare example of a fort turned functional winery.

Located in Trentino, an ancient wine-growing region of northern Italy, Noarna was converted to

Schloss Johannisberg GERMANY

24 WINERIES WITH STYLE

Schloss Johannisberg GERMANY

THE ICON APPROACH

Mönchhof GERMANY >> 31

winemaking in 1989. It is the latest development in the castle's long history – the fortified origins of the site date back to the Roman era, and echoes of past residents from prince-bishops to witches reverberate around its high roofs and sturdy walls. You are more likely to run into piles of barrels than damsels in distress in its sparse rooms these days, though. This might not appear to be the most practical of wineries, but those thick walls do act as excellent temperature and humidity regulators. Like ancient caves and cellars, old structures can serve new purposes.

Another medieval fortification sits at the heart of Schloss Vollrads in Germany's Rheingau region. It's more accurately described as a moated tower and was built around 1330 by the Greiffenclau family for protection against marauding bandits and pillagers who would sail up the river Rhine. They had moved there from the Graues Haus in Winkel, one of the oldest inhabited stone structures in Germany.

In its collective form, Vollrads is a little village in true estate style. Like Noarna, Vollrads has moved with the times, but here the extensions and alterations took place outside the tower, which had simply become too crowded after one generation sired an impressive twenty-six children. The stately building, in the compartmentalized cellars of which the wine is now made, was built in 1684; the latest building work took place in 2003 and more is planned.

Ongoing renovation, like the tower, is very much at the heart of Vollrads. "History is a burden," I was reminded when strolling around the property one summer's day, "but it can also give you a great sense of belonging." My thoughts turned to the last Greiffenclau after twenty-nine generations to own the estate, Erwein, who died in 1997. In the acquisition struggle that followed, the buildings, vineyards, and brand were in danger of being split. But they weren't – the value of what is described as the cradle and flagship of German wine could not be overlooked by the bank that now owns it.

"When we build let us think that we build for ever", wrote John Ruskin, the Victorian architecture critic and, as Hugh Johnson points out in his *Story of Wine*, son of a wine merchant. In his famous book, *The Seven Lamps of Architecture*, Ruskin defines a building's glory as "that deep sense of voicefulness […] which we feel in walls that have long been washed by the passing waves of humanity." Iconic wine estates have some of that quality – the stain of history that marks the cyclical revolutions of the wine-growing season.

Permanence in the midst of the shifting sands of history is something that Schloss Johannisberg has also achieved. Just up the road from Vollrads, it has an equally emblematic stature, though a quite different history. Religious, not secular in origin, its oldest cellars date back to when it was founded by Benedictine monks around AD 1100. And Johannisberg's revival is more than just figurative: on August 13, 1942, an Allied bombing raid razed the property to the ground.

Owner Princess Tatiana von Metternich likens her reaction to that of a castaway thrown on a beach after a huge storm. However, after she arrived in 1945 she wrote that the Rheingau "seemed to us to be an oasis of peace […] the towns sprang up out of rubble and ashes and wine 'gladdened men's hearts again.'" I caught up with the princess when she was leaving to catch the evening light for her customary watercolour session. Elegant in age and razor sharp in manner, she tells me about a book she is writing and describes turbulent, painful times in matter-of-fact terms. "It's important to remember," she says.

Motivated by recreating one of the most iconic estates in the Rheingau and all of Germany, along with her husband she rebuilt the property complete with its Benedictine church. The original 850-year-old cellars had, of course, survived, and are now as central to Johannisberg as the tower at Vollrads. The baroque palace is undoubtedly impressive – its commanding hilltop location over the Rhine is spectacular – but it's the cellar where the voicefulness and peace is most keenly felt. Wine matures in cask; bottles date back to 1748. On one of

WINERIES WITH STYLE

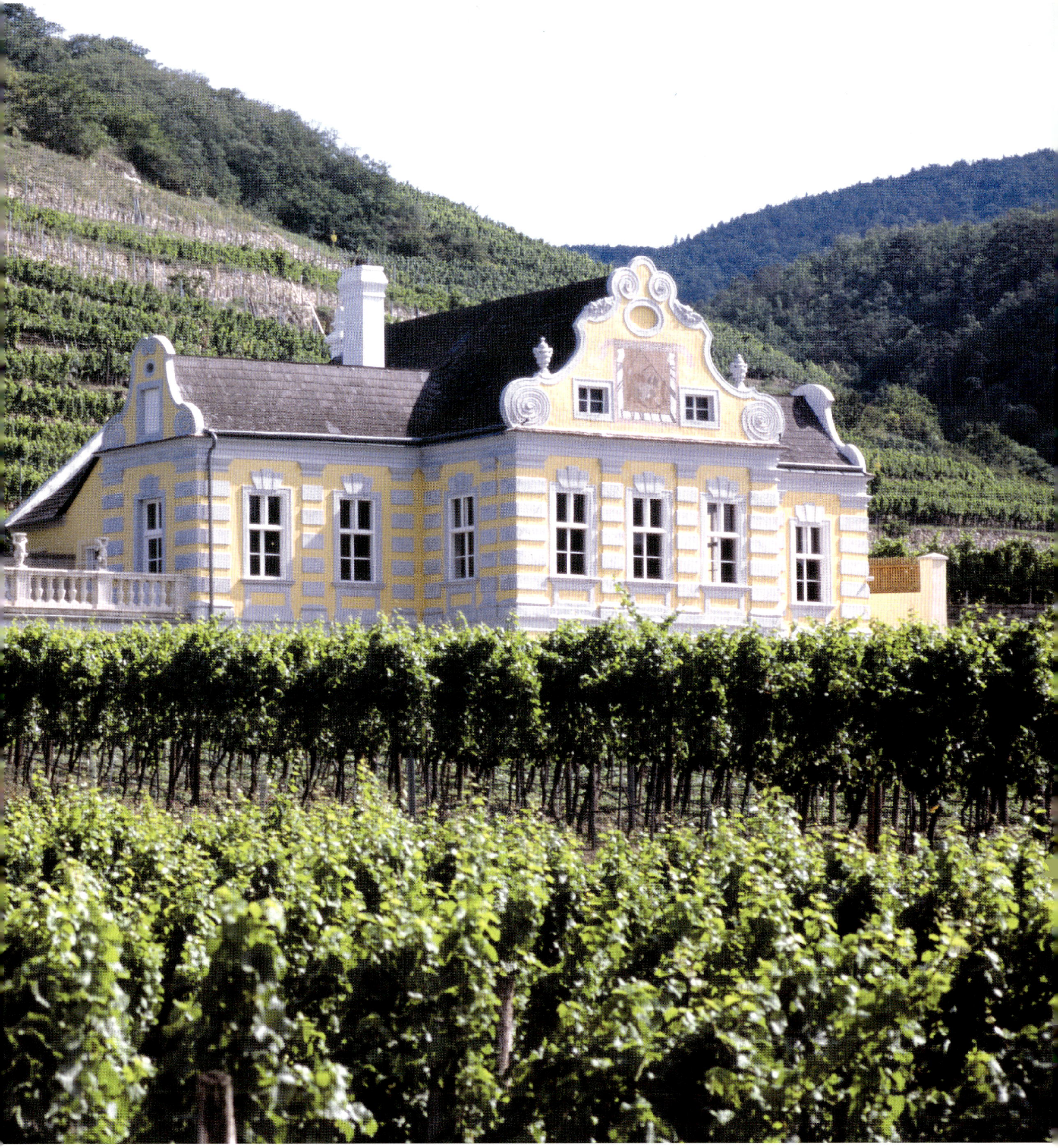

FWW AUSTRIA

the wooden vats is written a verse from Psalm 104. It reads, *"Et vinum laetificet cor hominis."* That is, "and wine to gladden men's hearts."

If Vollrads and Johannisberg have anything in common, it's a sense of constant evolution. It's there in the architecture as well as the wine: steady reinvention together with the weight of tradition. Wine has a canny way of outgrowing its confines. This can, of course, lead to as mass of ugly, sprawling buildings (unforgivable in modern wineries, betraying a simple lack of planning and inflexibility), but where it is carefully managed, it can be a harmonious evolution.

Religion was crucial to the development of wine in the Middle Ages. Without the organizing and educational influence of the religious communities, it is difficult to say whether wine would be where and what it is today; maybe we'd all be drinking beer instead. The classic example is the Cistercians in Burgundy, whose influence pretty much wrote the map of today's dizzyingly complex vineyard set-up. Religious communities, the Cistercians in particular, left significant architectural legacies; the language of religion still permeates wine, and especially its architecture. "Cathedrals" and "temples" of wine are common descriptions of wineries.

Revolutions and dissolutions, though, led to many monasteries and religious communities losing control of their vineyards and property after the Middle Ages. And change of ownership can often be more damaging to wine estates than to other businesses, because the most important assets are often lost in the change-over – that is, the wealth of experience and knowledge that is gained only with time and painstaking effort in the vineyard and winery.

It's rare, then, to find a religious community that has resisted such changes and continues to exist as a thriving wine estate. The Abbazia di Novacella is a fully functioning Augustinian monastery of thirty brothers, located beneath a skyline of Alpine peaks near Italy's Alto Adige Valley – also known by its Austrian name Südtirol. The Alpine feel is pervasive, from the crisp white wines to the newly converted cowshed that is Novacella's brand new winery. Seventy cows are ruing that decision.

But as with the other historic wine estates, Novacella has had to move with the times. Founded in 1142 by the Bishop of Brixen, Novacella used to be an important stopping point for pilgrims en route to the Holy Land or the Vatican. Now, however, the pilgrims are not the pious: they are tourists, relatives coming to pick up children from the Abbazia's school, or businessmen availing themselves of the latest in conference facilities. It is heartening that, amid all this modernizing, the magnificent baroque library and church, as well as the vaulted wine cellar, remain at the spiritual and aesthetic heart of the estate.

Self-promotion is, of course, the *raison d'être* of icons. Iconic wine estates adapt and change over time but ultimately succeed in retaining a coherent identity. One character might be more extrovert than the next; such is the case with Mönchhof in Germany's Mosel Valley.

The Mosel is a river that has carved a spectacular landscape of narrow banks and steep cliffs where vines hang on for dear life. In such a landscape, not many buildings stand out as immediately noticeable. Mönchhof, however, is one of them. Monastic is exactly what it doesn't seem, but believe it or not, Mönchhof was originally built by Cistercian monks – the cellars in the thirteenth century, the manor house in 1509.

In contrast to Novacella, here we have an example of secularization – and in flamboyant style. The building's striking façade was actually added in 1898 after the Eymael family had bought the estate from Napoleon at a Paris auction in 1804. Jean Eymael had made his money in textiles in Brazil and fancied adding a samba touch to the Mosel. "The façade," reads the winery's website, "has given the Mönchhof recognition far beyond the Mosel."

Not all the action takes place above ground at Mönchhof, however. Impressive cellars stretch underneath the manor house, but their precious contents face a constant threat: water. Humidity is generally encouraged in cellars to stop wood and cork drying out, but the Mosel has a tricky tendency to burst its banks once or twice every decade. That's too much water. "Ach, we just open the barrels," jokes Robert Eymael, patting one of the precious barrels in his gloomy cellar, a cool sanctuary even during one of the hottest days of the year. "It's why our wines go so well with fish."

Staatlicher Hofkeller Würzburg GERMANY

THE ICON APPROACH

32 WINERIES WITH STYLE

Staatlicher Hofkeller Würzburg GERMANY >>35

THE ICON APPROACH

The light-hearted, flamboyant approach is also very much in evidence at Freie Weingärtner Wachau (FWW) in Austria. Even its location, on the slopes in the narrow Danube valley in the Wachau region, is reminiscent of Mönchhof. It, too, was commissioned by a monastery, the work of the celebrated Baroque architect Jakob Prandtauer. And while it has been renovated but not significantly altered since it was built around 1715, it is the mixture of playfulness and gravity that makes this building so intriguing.

The Kellerschlössel, as FWW's spiritual headquarters is known, is true to its name – a small manor house (*schlössel*) over a cellar (*keller*). The latter follows a labyrinthine course sixteen metres (fifty-three feet) underground, where the serious business of maturing wine is undertaken. But above ground, the vivid building's main gable sports a solar dial and fresco of carousing gentlemen. Inside, decorations abound on wine; satirical, religious, and humorous themes in a unique collection of graphic art. It's pure entertainment, albeit with a serious undertone.

In this sense, we come back to the idea of vines being rooted but wine being able to set the spirit soaring, as Irene Johner so eloquently put it. This is a serious business – the FWW is a cooperative, with 740 members to take care of, in a demanding and cost-intensive landscape – but the image, the welcome, is all lightness and play.

Architects sometimes compare the shape of a winery to a vine – the cellars like roots, the buildings like a canopy. Acknowledging nature's input implies a certain humility on the part of a designer, just as it does with a winemaker. It means the ego is not all-consuming; an open mind is able to learn, improve, better itself, and work in tandem with nature, with often beneficial results for wine as well as architecture.

That attitude has not always been evident in mankind's history. In architectural terms, a contrasting, totalitarian attitude toward the environment can be seen set in stone, halls of mirrors, and regimented garden-work at Versailles, Louis XIV's very own tower of Babel. Its effect is not subtle; it is simply meant to blow you away. Château Margaux (*see* p.20) is often referred to as the Versailles of the wine world. This is quite wrong. Margaux has a serene, self-contained dignity; Versailles is about pomp and ostentation. In fact, the wine world's closest relation to Versailles can be found not in France but in Germany. More specifically, in Germany's Bavarian heartlands, an area (ironically) better known for its beer-swilling than for its wine.

We have already come across the Greiffenclau family at Schloss Vollrads (*see* p.27), itself an imposing piece of wine architecture. And we have seen flourishes of baroque flamboyance at the likes of Mönchhof and FWW. The Staatlicher Hofkeller in Würzburg, however, and the palatial *residenz* that crowns its cellars, is related – but in another league.

Apart from its generally colossal stature, one of the most striking parts of the property is the main staircase. Karl-Philipp von Greiffenclau, one of the prince-bishops of Würzburg who orchestrated this marvel, had perhaps been scarred by the memory of cramped moated towers at Vollrads. He commissioned Giovanni Battista Tiepolo to paint one of the world's largest ceiling frescoes, suspended above an already fantastically elaborate staircase, that was festooned with statues and ornament.

If you follow the stairs down instead of up, however, you come to cellars that manage to be almost as palatial as the *residenz* above. Unlike the *residenz*, this part of the property serves its original purpose. Wine is still made here, today by Bavaria's state domain, and as a roomy but practical space, it helps dilute the scale of the ostentation above.

A similar grounding of grandeur in the reality of winemaking can be found in a somewhat less expected environment: the Crimea. The Massandra winery was built on the orders of Tsar Nicholas II, who wanted nothing less than the "best winery in the world" to keep his summer residence in wine. A suitably grand edifice was duly erected, but the real business took place underground, where Georgian miners were busied constructing three levels of cellars, each level well over a kilometre (more than a half-mile) long.

A famous architect once described architecture as history in stone. The Crimea is not short on history – notable events include the Charge of the Light Brigade and the Yalta Conference that redefined world order in the wake of World War II – and Massandra carries those marks of the past in its stone. After its inception as an imperial winery in the 1890s, its unique collection of wine was hidden from Bolsheviks and Nazis to survive today as some one million bottles of its own and others' wines, with bottles dating back to 1775. The hammer and sickle still hang on its stolid façade, the most visible gesture to times past.

Wine is no longer made at Massandra, but its cellars are still in service. Parts of its collection of predominantly sweet and fortified wines (boasting labels such as Bastardo, Black Doctor, Crimean White Port and Sunny Valley) have been up for sale at Sotheby's auction house. It is described in Jancis Robinson and Hugh Johnson's *The World Atlas of*

Massandra UKRAINE

Cos d'Estournel FRANCE

Wine as "the world's largest and certainly most distinctive, collection of old wines". The Tsar created Massandra as a winery in the modern sense of the word. What had been a small element of a larger estate was being invested with a new importance in its own right; wine was inheriting its own architecture.

In Bordeaux, the château was traditionally separate from the *chai* and *cuvier* (the actual wineries) where the wine was made. The château was the grand part; it was what conferred gravity onto the product by association. Château Margaux (*see* p.20) is a fine example of this, even though its *chais* are, somewhat exceptionally, striking in their own right. By and large, wine buildings were simple and functional. The château did the talking.

The success of this icon approach, however, led to the term "château" being adopted as a sort of synonym for "good quality wine-producing estate", even by estates that had no château to speak of, or by wineries that were the other side of the world from Bordeaux. The phantom château was born, nothing more than a marketing ploy, an imaginary currency. The architecture of wine had entered mythical realms – the very notion of the château became nebulous, like a legendary tale that leaves you impressed but unconvinced.

There were those, however, who did things differently. What if, instead of dealing with all these disparate elements, you simply amalgamate the architectural aspiration of the château and the functionality of a wine building? That was the Tsar's bidding at Massandra; it was also the rationale behind Bordeaux's Cos d'Estournel.

Estournel, for all its light-hearted appearance, is a serious milestone in the evolution of wine and its architecture. It marks a point where wine is given a prominence it has enjoyed only fleetingly until now. There is no château, no manor house at Cos d'Estournel – nothing to detract from the wine, which takes centre stage, wrapped in oriental finery. What you see is nothing more than a winery.

Imagine walking through the elaborate archway crowned by heraldry, with a unicorn and lion rampant. "*Semper fidelis*", the motto reads. Pagoda-style towers rise up over an elaborate façade, in which is set an intricately carved door that once swung in a sultan's palace in Zanzibar. And inside… no sultans or harems, no lords and ladies, just wine. It's a powerful statement.

What it signifies is a shift away from an old order, in which wine was part of a greater aristocratic or religious estate, into a more focused, commercially driven environment in which wine takes precedence. To get too caught up in the exotic, melodramatic theatre of the building is to miss the point – it's a carefully contrived commercial tool, just like many châteaux before it but only now more defined in its role. (The oriental touches are simply historical context – the nineteenth century saw many European pastiches of so-called exotic design as the world opened up in a new era of travel. Margaux's Egyptian touches are another case in point.)

The world of wine is a constantly evolving and changing one. Each vintage gives different wines; human influence comes and goes; wines change over time in the bottle. It is a world in which experiencing the moment has a particular poignancy. The value of great wine architecture, though, is that it lends a sense of permanence to this artistry, and can be enjoyed in combination with, or independently from, the wine. It adds to the experience, but is also an experience in its own right.

In a way, Cos d'Estournel set the scene for many modern wineries. Not in its exotic drapery (though many Californian wineries might beg to differ) but in the very concept of the iconic winery, as distinct from a wine estate. This threw up many new challenges, not least how to infuse the very specific functional requirements of winemaking with the spirit of great architecture. It's a challenge that has met with many intriguing solutions.

Cos d'Estournel FRANCE >> 36

IN BRIEF

CHATEAU MARGAUX
Margaux, Bordeaux, France
BUILT c.1810 by Louis Combes
WINE TIP 1999 vintage
VISITS By appointment
www.chateau-margaux.com

While few wines can be described as sobering, Château Margaux is sobriety in stone. Its wine is among the finest in Bordeaux, if not the world; its château typifies this serene majesty. "It's good to share this with people – we're proud," says winemaker Paul Pontallier modestly. Second label Pavillon is also classy stuff, both red and white.

VILLA DI MASER
Montello e Colli Asolani, Veneto, Italy
BUILT 1550s by Andrea Palladio
WINE TIP Il Maserino Merlot
VISITS Open doors
www.villadimaser.it

Owner Vittorio Dalle Ore describes Maser as "a joy". I couldn't agree more. Palladio's villa is so precious that over-shoe slippers are obligatory inside lest the footwear of eager visitors damage the precious floors. The wine labels sport the villa's original sixteenth century architectural plan, but you'll only ever feel the genius on site.

CHATEAU KSARA
Bekaa Valley, Lebanon
BUILT 1857
WINE TIP Réserve du Couvent
VISITS Open doors
www.ksara.com.lb

Ksara is far from being the world's most impressive winery, but it does offer a glimpse into wine's rich history. Its land is close to where wine is first thought to have emerged; Roman tunnels evoke ancient civilizations; its religious associations point to wine's close affinity with the church. Intrigued by how the wines taste? You should be.

CASTEL NOARNA
Trentino, Italy
BUILT Eleventh century onwards
WINE TIP Romeo
VISITS Open doors
www.castelnoarna.com

Vineyards now lie on the dauntingly steep slopes that any attacker would have had to scale to penetrate these formidable defences. This atmospheric ancient fortification traces its origins back to Roman times and has seen some history since. Not least of which was being converted into a working winery in 1989.

SCHLOSS VOLLRADS
Rheingau, Germany
BUILT 1330 onwards
WINE TIP Riesling Edition
VISITS Open doors
www.schlossvollrads.com

To this day treasures are kept inside Vollrads' medieval architecture, such as one of the first-ever printed books, dating from 1463 (printing was invented just across the Rhine in Mainz by Gutenberg in the 1450s). After a period of instability, Vollrads' wines are now aiming to regain their rightful place among Germany's most prestigious, although this takes time.

SCHLOSS JOHANNISBERG
Rheingau, Germany
BUILT 1100 onwards
WINE TIP Schloss Johannisberg Spätlese
VISITS Open doors
www.schloss-johannisberg.de

Classic, pure, subtle, elegant – such are Johannisberg's superb wines. They're some of Germany's finest, and the estate itself has also become something of an icon. Its long and eventful history takes in figures such as Charlemagne, Napoleon, Thomas Jefferson, and Yehudi Menuhin. It enjoys a commanding position above the Rhine.

ABBAZIA DI NOVACELLA
Isarco Valley, Italy
BUILT 1142 onwards
WINE TIP Praepositus Kerner
VISITS Open doors
www.kloster-neustift.it

Most medieval monasteries have long since given up the religious ghost and gone secular. Not Novacella. It's still a fully functioning and rapidly modernizing community of Augustinian monks. You might expect the wines to play second fiddle to all this, but no. They're excellent – the outrageously exotic Rosenmuskateller is compulsory tasting.

MONCHHOF
Mosel-Saar-Ruwer, Germany
BUILT Thirteenth century onwards
WINE TIP Würzgarten Spätlese
VISITS By appointment
www.moenchhof.de

Mönchhof is a big pink cupcake of a building surrounded by steep green vineyards. It's quite a scene. Owner Robert Eymael also controls the smaller Christoffel Erben estate, but for both he aims to make wines with "marvellous fruit and great clarity". They show promise.

FWW
Wachau, Austria
BUILT 1715 by Jakob Prandtauer
WINE TIP Grüner Veltliner Smaragd Achleiten
VISITS Open doors
www.fww.at

Originally built for the Dürnstein monastery, FWW's iconic *kellerschlössel* building is now, after a recent refurbishment, a mini-museum and shop. FWW is a cooperative cellar and one of the best of its kind, producing some outstanding Austrian wine.

STAATLICHER HOFKELLER WURZBURG
Franken, Germany
BUILT 1744 by Balthasar Neumann
WINE TIP Rieslaner Auslese
VISITS Open doors
www.hofkeller.de

"It's all about baroque sensuality," was how Hofkeller's spectacular surroundings were described to me. In the eighteenth century the prince-bishops of Würzburg left their castle and built a palace to rival Versailles. Cavernous cellars were needed to pay the multitude of servants, noblemen and clergy in wine. The architecture is stunning; the wines pale somewhat by comparison.

MASSANDRA
Crimea, Ukraine
BUILT 1890s
VISITS Open doors
www.massandra.crimea.com

Although wine is no longer made at Massandra, it is still stored in what is a living testament to the rich history of the Crimea and its winemaking traditions. Its unique collection of wines began under Tsar Nicolas II and was later shielded from both Bolsheviks and Nazis. Massandra wines are still made by its sister wineries all along what is known as the Crimean Côte d'Azur.

COS D'ESTOURNEL
St-Estèphe, Bordeaux, France
BUILT c.1830
WINE TIP 1985 vintage
VISITS By appointment
www.cosestournel.com

Cos is a little island of funky exoticism amid the traditional heartland of Bordeaux. Palm trees, pagodas, triumphal arches, a mock medieval tower, ornate stonework – and all to the glory of wine. The wine, by contrast, is a combination of power and austerity, a regular star of its commune St-Estèphe and a shining light in Bordeaux.

Château Margaux FRANCE

Cos d'Estournel FRANCE

Château Ksara LEBANON

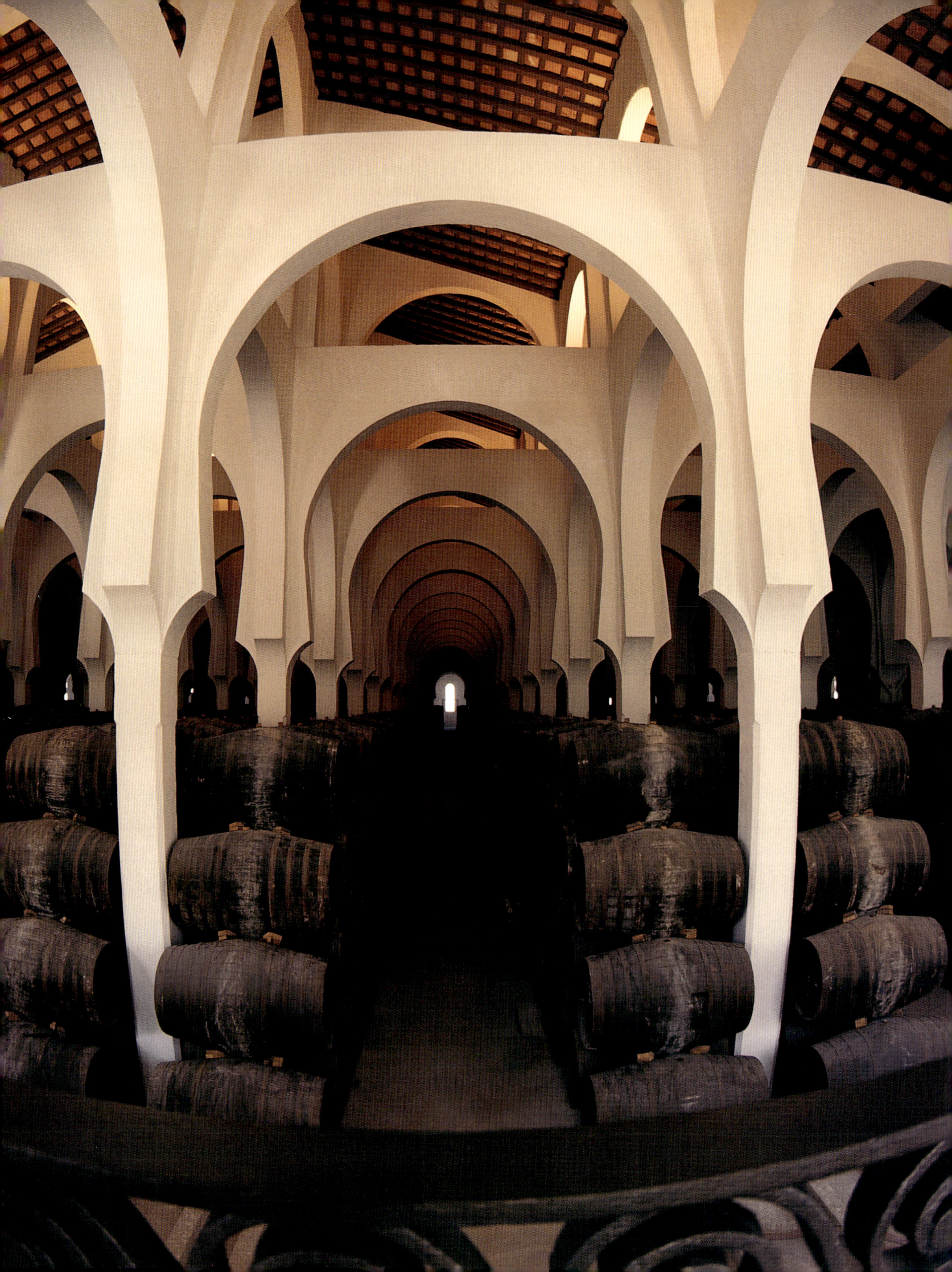

SOUNDS OF THE UNDERGROUND

THE LABYRINTHINE WORLD OF THE WINE CELLAR

Wine is happiest and safest in the cool, dark surroundings of the cellar. As a result, many wineries have gone underground, often with extraordinary results. As Prince Alain de Polignac, a descendant of Champagne's Madame Pommery, said, "Writing would reinvent itself to express the magic of these places."

Pommery FRANCE

When Theseus was thrown into the labyrinth, he knew that somewhere in its dark recesses stalked the vicious Minotaur – half human, half bull – ready to devour him. Failing that, he would surely die lost in the labyrinth. But Theseus knew the secret to getting out alive – a ball of thread tied to the entrance would enable him to retrace his steps and escape. How did he know? The tip came from the ingenious architect who had built the labyrinth in the first place: Daedalus.

We remember the mythological Daedalus most fondly as the father who tried in vain to stop his son Icarus flying too close to the sun. But it was as an architect, inventor, and sculptor that he earned his name – Daedalus is Latin for "skilfully wrought". His labyrinth, from which escape was impossible, earned fame throughout the world.

Labyrinthine is a word often used to describe the world of wine. There are two reasons why such a term is apt: firstly, wine in all its myriad incarnations has to be one of the most bewilderingly complex subjects you can fit into a glass. Secondly, it's a word that speaks evocatively of the murky subterranean world of the wine cellar. Escape is possible, of course, though with some of the world's largest wine cellars stretching up to thirty kilometres (more than eighteen miles) underground, it's not always obvious.

Dark, silent, damp, and cool is wine's idea of bliss. Its sensitive chemistry can easily be spoiled by harsh conditions; the simplest remedy is often found in underground spaces. Renaissance architect Andrea Palladio's sixteenth century prescription for wine cellars was that they be "underground, enclosed, and far away from commotion, humidity, or smell." By and large it's sound advice; but it's not the only way.

As with all things in wine, it's about striking the right balance to suit the given circumstances. Good wine is about expressing local character, a sense of origin –

42   WINERIES WITH STYLE

Pommery FRANCE >>47

Pommery FRANCE

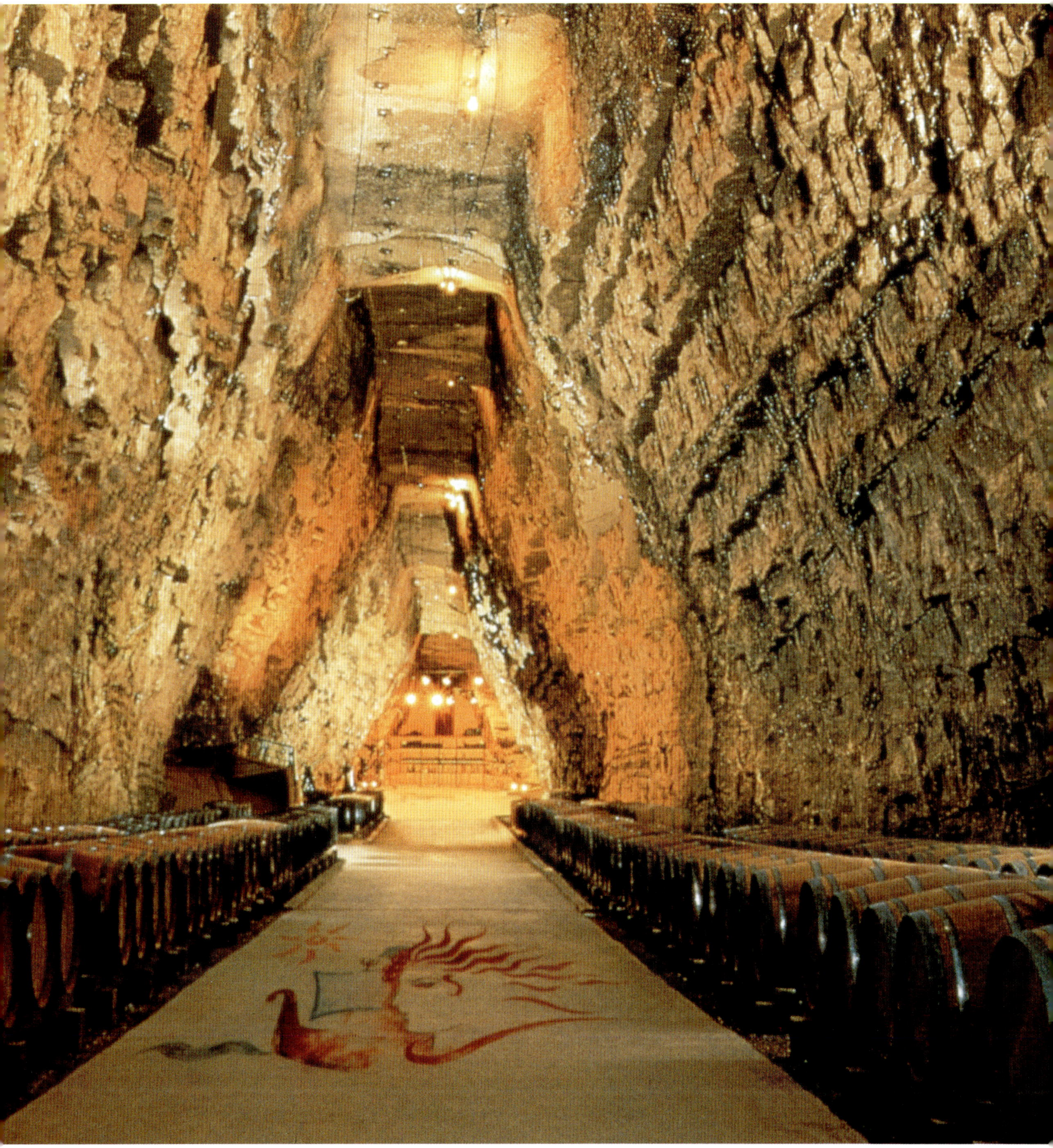

this is what stops wine becoming bland and industrialized. That origin is often thought of simply as referring to the vineyard, but in certain cases it also applies to how the wine is made or matured and, by extension, the buildings where winemaking takes place.

Sherry is made in Spain's dusty, dry south. On first impressions, it hardly seems fine wine country. Too hot, too dry, too harsh. Then you notice the details. The chalk-white *albariza* soil reflects the sun, protecting water below. Breezes sail in off the Atlantic to the west. And the bodegas, or barrel halls, where the sherry is matured, are specifically engineered to suit the wine: precise orientation, siting, and design are crucial to enable the wine to mature in its special way – and the quality of sherry is just as much about how it is matured as its raw ingredients.

This is where the sherry bodega differs with Palladio. In a hot, dry climate, establishing balance (in this case the special conditions for sherry maturation) means encouraging humidity and harnessing sea breezes above ground. Precise northwest southeast orientation, small high windows covered with esparto grass, high ceilings, and thick walls all aim to bring in the breeze, retain humidity and ward off the sun. All this ensures a slow, complex ageing process. It's the underground brought overground. The result is often monumental.

Sherry bodegas are frequently described as cathedrals. Domecq's bodega, by contrast, was christened La Mezquita (mosque) because its architect saw in the bodega's very specific requirements an opportunity to reflect the Islamic architecture so characteristic of the region. (Moors had come to Spain from North Africa as early as AD711, inspiring a fertile cross-fertilization of culture, especially in the south). The inspiration was the famous eighth century mosque in nearby Córdoba. There, a forest of columns and double horseshoe arches creates a sense of harmony and infinity. Domecq's La Mezquita has more arches than its teetotal model and creates the same impression of calm divinity.

Château Ausone FRANCE >>47–8

Château Ausone FRANCE

Like sherry, Champagne is a fussy adolescent. Its secret is just as reliant on a special, often lengthy, ageing process – which makes it sparkle – and this maturation period means that producers have to keep large stockholdings. And like sherry, Champagne is also grown on chalky soils. The difference is that in the cooler climate of Champagne, what are chalky soils for the vines also double up as chalky walls for some of the most atmospheric underground cellars ever seen.

It was the Romans who started quarrying the Champagne chalk for building materials. As the city of Reims and its kind grew, so great pits were sunk into the earth. Once abandoned, however, these sites quickly became derelict. When Madame Pommery, one of Champagne's very own breed of stalwart widows, decided to use the land in 1868 to create a striking new base for her Champagne firm Pommery, the works were conducted on a colossal scale.

Some 120 Gallo-Roman chalk pits were joined and extended by no less than eighteen kilometres (eleven miles) of high-vaulted galleries, reaching a depth of thirty metres (ninety-eight feet) below ground level. As Pommery went about the business of making Champagne, more than 100 permanent workers were employed in these subterranean passages alone. A single staircase of 116 steps is the passageway to this cavernous domain; once below, sculptures and bas-reliefs throw exaggerated shadows to add a touch of theatre to proceedings.

The impression of industry is clearly evident at Pommery. Not just in the sheer scale of the operation, but in the nature of its construction, and this is what makes its charm all the more notable. The original pits were simple quarries and, although their excavators are long gone, new tunnels built and bottles installed, the feel of a working mine is never too distant.

Reinvention is a constant theme in the architecture of wine – castles and cowsheds can be adapted to winemaking just as ancient design can be taken up and revamped in the most modern structures. At its most basic, though, this reinvention consists of a magpie-like appropriation of disused structures. What lies beneath is usually immune from the demolition gang; abandoned mines lend themselves to wine easily enough. Three very different French examples of such vinous requisitions are Pommery, Terra-Vinéa in Corbières, and Château Ausone in Bordeaux.

A small path snakes through the scrub and stone of Mediterranean Corbières above the warm patchwork of tiled roofs that is Portel. This is a different world from the grass and chill of Champagne; unrelated to the undulating aristocracy of Bordeaux. The light is bright and pure, Mediterranean, the land convulsed and fierce. Geology seems alive in such an environment, and you realize that the vines are not the only ones able to experience it as the path ends in an immaculate timber-framed gallery that leads precipitously down into the rock. This is the earth at first hand.

Terra-Vinéa is an old gypsum mine where the cooperative cellar Caves Rocbère now matures its wine from the surrounding regions of Corbières and Fitou, as well as further afield. Gypsum, or calcium sulphate, is used in plastering and has also, coincidentally, found previous employment in the vinification of sherry. The excavations have left ample space, not just for resonant barrel hollows but also, in unusually tourist-hungry fashion for the French, various mannequin-addled recreations of times past. "We want people to come and experience our heritage," says Rocbère's Vianney Castan. He explains about the area's rich Roman history and, more recently, how when the mine recently closed down after 200 years' work, it was given to Rocbère. "It's not very practical," he concedes, "but this was the heart and soul of the village – everyone worked here and wine was just a weekend job. So when it shut we were determined to make it live again." Subsidies were sought and won to shore up the structure and the local wine found an amenable cellar. Once again, change had looked kindly on wine.

Château Ausone is similar to Rocbère and Pommery in having commandeered an old excavation site, but there the similarity ends. Ausone is a tiny operation

SOUNDS OF THE UNDERGROUND 47

Redi ITALY >>48

by Bordeaux standards, producing a mere 2,200-odd cases of highly prized wine a year, some of the best the region has to offer. The bustling, photogenic town of St-Emilion sits no more than a stone's throw away and there is a similar feel of confined profusion about Ausone. A vineyard and thirteenth century chapel perch directly above the cellar, whose entrance is set Ali Baba-style in the rock face. It's as if the vines' roots find nourishment in the cellar itself.

When I visited, construction work was going on all around, under the dogged eye of owner Alain Vauthier. "I don't think wine buildings should be too permanent or entrenched," says Vauthier. "Ideas and techniques are always changing and you don't want to be bogged down." Even the Bordeaux elite moves on. We step into the thoroughly atmospheric cellars, which have been extensively renovated. Chalk shavings cover the floor; Alain murmurs something about "aromatic purity".

It may be the sudden gloom, but Vauthier's eyes seem to burn even brighter. "A good cellar is not a fridge, nor an iron cage," he pauses, perhaps searching for the right words, perhaps assessing my reaction. "It's a place of tranquility. Often, it's just logic, respecting nature, getting the orientation right. I want an emotional charge, a sense of comfort, like the kind of feeling you have in a church."

An excellent definition of the rationale behind wine cellars comes courtesy of Italian producers Redi, in Montepulciano. Redi's elegant, high-vaulted cellars are described by writer Piero Zoi as "a true wine temple, where in sacred silence… the wine undergoes a particular process which only precious woody essences and time can give." It's good because it doesn't attempt to simplify what is a complex process in which time and tranquility are crucial ingredients.

Redi was based on designs drawn up by Baldassare Peruzzi, one of the finest Renaissance architects in Rome, who had worked with Raphael and Bramante on St Peter's. He died before work was complete on Redi, however, and it is thought that as the site is on a sharp slope, the builders may have further excavated the cellar to help level out the height of the austere palazzo above. It is certainly a cavernous cellar space, yet with a particularly Italian elegance, lofty and graceful, the artistry blended with natural forms where brickwork intertwines with the chiselled boulder on which the palazzo rests.

For wine, though, the effect of time can be detrimental as well as beneficial. Even the best wine can pass its peak; vines die of old age; knowledge can pass away. One winery attempting to reverse the march of history is Mastroberardino, in the ancient heartland of top Roman viticulture, Campania.

Antonio and Piero Mastroberardino cultivate grape varieties that were used by the Romans, at a location a short distance from Pompeii. In Hugh Johnson's *Story of Wine*, he notes how Pompeii had "foreshadowed" Bordeaux with its dominance of the international wine trade and the "splendid villas" that surrounded the town. The villas, as he eloquently puts it, "were the châteaux of their day, their vineyards lapping their walls, their cellars full of maturing wine." Pompeii was obviously fond of a drink – Bacchic murals and bars crop up all over the ancient town's ruins – and not only the wine but also the architectural legacy is captured in Mastroberardino's fine buildings and barrel-vaulted cellars, where ceiling frescoes seem to add a special historic dimension to the space.

Piero Mastroberardino sums it up when he says, "more than an influence on the way we make our wines, architecture is an expression of the way we feel about the wine, its mission and role in the quality of life." In this regard, it is no surprise to hear him talk of the winery as "an institution, a symbol, and place where cultural and family values are preserved and transmitted to the future generations."

The architecture of the wine cellar is not all about preservation and keeping with tradition, however. González-Byass is one of the oldest and largest firms in the sherry business, yet it has managed to stay nimbly ahead of the game by a subtle combination of sound winemaking and shrewd marketing. Such a far-sighted strategy has involved commissioning emblematic cellars by architects

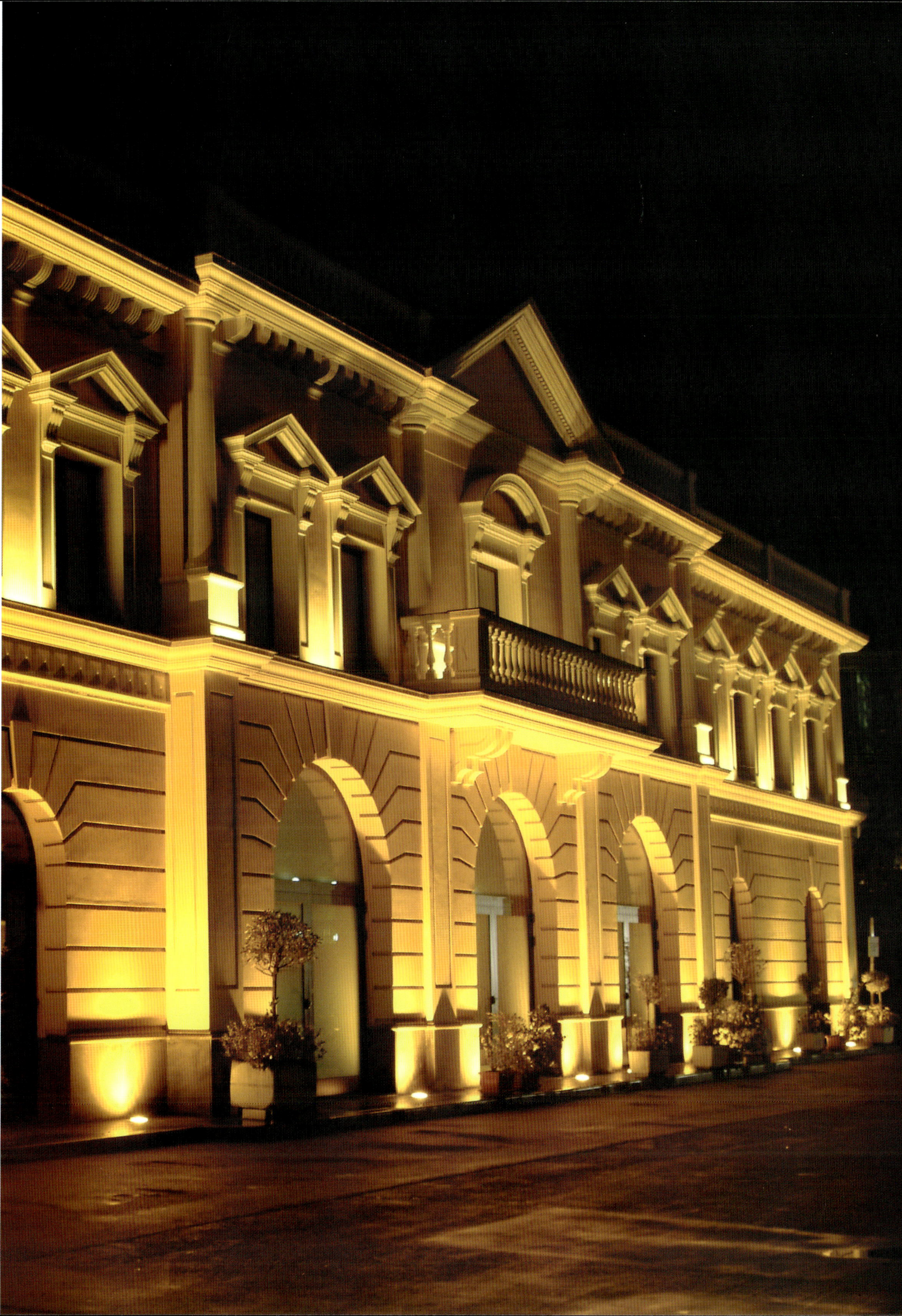

who were ahead of their time, yet who respected the very specific requirements of the sherry bodega.

Las Copas was built by J.A. Torroja Cavanillas, son of the famous pioneering concrete engineer who had built González-Byass' Gran Bodega a decade before. It was constructed around the same time as Domecq's La Mezquita in the early 1970s, but where the latter is retrospective, Las Copas is *avant-garde*. Hundreds of geometric cupolas are interspersed with inverted equivalents that double up as rain-water recyclers. Its light, strong, almost impudent structure is a deliberate move away from sherry tradition.

Innovation was nothing new for González-Byass, though. Gustave Eiffel had built La Concha more than a century earlier, a circular, clear-span roofed bodega that was itself ground-breaking in its lack of supports and steel girder frame. This was the time of the Industrial Revolution, a new age of architecture and human endeavour, symbolized by Eiffel's Parisian tower, which he described as "the resounding proof of the progress achieved this century by the art of engineers". Eiffel captures that buzz in La Concha, and its avant-garde design not only points to the dawning era of mass production and mass marketing, but also a new dimension in wine architecture.

If wine and its architecture have had two heydays in the modern age it would be the mid-nineteenth century and the 1980s onwards. On both occasions, the revolution was in part an underground affair. Eiffel provided some international architectural prestige for González-Byass and its cellars in 1862; Catalan architect Ricardo Bofill did exactly the same thing for Château Lafite-Rothschild in 1987. It was to prove trend-setting.

Lafite supremo Eric de Rothschild had worked out that by arranging barrels in a circular fashion instead of the customary rectangular layout in Bordeaux *chais*, significant time and energy could be saved in the winemaking process. Bofill came up with an octagonal concrete cellar with barrels arranged in concentric circles around a central, colonnaded skylight. It gives the impression of being a stage in the round with no actors, the barrels silent spectators. But it's practicality, not drama, that governed the design.

Being entirely underground, the cellar was naturally insulated and therefore more practical and economical to run. Moreover, its sunken location gave de Rothschild an idea – what with land (for vineyards as well as building) being so expensive in Bordeaux, why not get two for the price of one? The vineyard would be grafted on top of the buried building. Bofill's cellar has been compared to a theatre, mausoleum, and cathedral, but in the architect's own analogy, the concept is surely closer to a crypt, where wine awaits its fate by providing the foundations for vines up above.

Just a year later, in Bofill's Catalan homeland, an architect named Domingo Triay was putting the finishing touches to a startling structure on the vast, commissions. But I'm not sure I buy the line about Raimat's "impeccable integration".

What makes Raimat intriguing is not just the architect's hide-the-winery routine (which arguably works better in Codorníu and Triay's Californian winery, Artesa), it's the way Triay has pitted his vision against tradition. Raimat's original winery, near to the new building but very much a separate structure, was built in 1918 by Rubió i Bellver, a contemporary of Catalan master architect Antoni Gaudí. Its broad, smooth arches – reputedly the first use of reinforced concrete in Spain – reflect some of the modernist obsession with natural forms and curved lines. The roof is stepped, not only to allow light to filter through but also because Bellver originally wanted water to cascade down the roof as a form of natural refrigeration.

This somewhat fanciful waterfall roof is translated into the vineyard covering on Triay's modern structure, but instead of harmony with the landscape the impression here is of a seething cauldron of modernity that disappears reluctantly under the earth. Immaculate white columns, glass panelling, polished surfaces, angular lines – the landscape doesn't know what's hit it. Even the reflective lake out front is out of place in this desert environment. It's a stunning addition to the winemaking site, but more in terms of its boldness than any sort of brushing under a landscape carpet.

Three of Codorníu's wineries are grouped here because they represent a progression of an architectural style (in this case, in an underground setting) that seems to stay remarkably fresh and provocative over time. The company's most emblematic structure is its headquarters in Sant Sadurní d'Anoia, at the heart of the Catalan region where cava as we know it now was first developed and commercialized in the late nineteenth century. At the forefront of that charge was the Raventós family, owners of Codorníu.

Cava went down a storm with a public drunk on industrial success and economic prosperity. In Catalonia, it was a time of social and artistic renaissance – Gaudí was leading the architectural charge, his vision of contorted yet functional natural forms infectious. When Manuel Raventós came to build a winery, he wanted not only an ambitious, spacious cellar; he was far-sighted enough to want to capture the prevailing spirit of strong, imaginative Catalan identity.

Josep Puig i Cadafalch, along with Gaudí one of the prime exponents of Spanish *modernismo*, designed a series of four buildings in just such a style for Codorníu. The scale, however, was immense, characterized by sweeping arches and cavernous halls, the parabolic designs repeated daintily on the

wind-swept Raimat estate. It, too, was a modern winery, with a vineyard for a roof. Building it had involved a hill being levelled, the land excavated, developed, and then re-covered with soil, grass, and vines. A glittering façade of glass and white columns protrudes from the earth. It was, in the company's words, "impeccable integration into the landscape".

The company in question is Codorníu, a large Spanish wine group with wineries all over the world, but based in Catalonia and a stalwart of cava, Spain's famous fizz. The Codorníu group is a treasure trove of architectural interest in wine terms and deserves praise for its commitment to brave and innovative buildings's exterior along with distinctive ceramic mosaics. Like an iceberg, though, Codorníu's real bulk lies underground – on five subterranean levels, its labyrinthine cellars extend over thirty kilometres (nineteen miles). Even Pommery (see p.47) is small fry compared to this.

In the early days, Spanish sparkling wine was known as "Champagne" (*Champán*) – but when legal requirements forced them to come up with a more original name, they went underground. In *The New Spain*, John Radford points out that while the Spanish words "bodega" and "cava" both mean cellar, the former refers to structures above ground and the latter those below. As cava, like Champagne, undergoes a period of cellar ageing to gain its fizz, it is usually stocked in some quantity below ground and when it is ready, it is taken from the cava. Spanish fizz had a new name born of its underground architecture.

Cadafalch's creation was one of many such modernist wine cellars that spread across Catalonia at that time – Raimat is another, subsequent, example. Codorníu, it seems, has been quite adept at starting trends, in architecture as well as wine. The influence even spread overseas when Domingo Triay collaborated with Californian architects Bouligny to create a new winery in California's Napa County just a year after he had finished building Raimat's brand new underground facility. Artesa, as it would come to be known, was almost identical in its quirky conception to Raimat.

When I went to visit Artesa, I drove straight past it. Twice. This is integration in the landscape taken to extremes. Artesa is built on top of a hill with commanding views, but where you might expect a grandiose architectural statement, instead you find a winery that has become part of the hill, hidden in the landscape. During construction, the hilltop was levelled, the winery built then soil and grass replanted, in similar fashion to Raimat. The only clues to Artesa's existence from the lower land are the dark tinted windows peeping out from what appears an innocuous hillside. At a glance, they look like rocks. Anyway, that was my excuse for arriving late.

Artesa is a potent statement. Wine is about capturing and expressing all that the local land has to offer, and wineries often strive to harmonize with the land in their turn. But Artesa surpasses that – it *is* the land. There are other fine examples in California of so-called invisible architecture, but Artesa is among the most extreme. Codorníu's underground ambitions reached a climax of sorts here.

Château Lafite-Rothschild FRANCE >>51

54 WINERIES WITH STYLE

Raimat SPAIN >>52

SOUNDS OF THE UNDERGROUND

Codorníu SPAIN >>52-3

Codorníu SPAIN

"I wanted a big winery, but not one that would traumatize the environment too much," says bustling, petite winemaker Elena Adel. These are not wholly unexpected words, except for the fact that Adel works not in Artesa but for the gargantuan Juan Alcorta winery in Rioja. Talking comparative ballparks, Artesa produces something in the region of a million litres of wine per year. Juan Alcorta makes twenty-four million. It is quite some achievement, then, that Alcorta's architect Ignacio Quemada has managed to bury the vinous equivalent of the Titanic. "We took advantage of a small ravine and then excavated some more," explains Adel. "If this were above ground, it would be enormous."

The sheer scale of Alcorta, like Pommery (see p.47) and Codorníu (see p.52), is staggering; the fact that such space and technological pyrotechnics exist underground is hard to grasp. The impact is largely engineered by the way you approach the winery above ground, past vineyards and vegetation, in through

SOUNDS OF THE UNDERGROUND

Artesa USA >>53

Artesa USA

low-slung, unobtrusive pastel buildings. Nothing special here, you think. And then you descend. Juan Alcorta is far from being the most beautiful or arresting winery in the world; its effect is cumulative. It's in the strange combination of an unashamedly industrial scale with an attention to detail, such as the pinpoint lighting and subtle colouring in the tank room, or the delicate ridging on the earthy hues of the exterior stonework. As Adel comments: "the architect looks for what's beautiful; we remind him what's practical. As in all things, it's about balance."

Balance is also central to the appeal of Salentein, a winery located high in Argentina's Andean foothills. At ground level, the winery is in the form of a cross, a series of four stern rectangles housing the modern vinification facilities under a simple, metal roof. It's nothing out of the ordinary, perhaps even a little dull in its symmetry and practicality. But where the winery comes alive is at the focal

SOUNDS OF THE UNDERGROUND

point of the building, its epicentre, where a large circular opening drops eighteen metres (sixty feet) into an underground cellar that takes the hard lines of technology and transforms them into an almost religious space (see p.62).

The central, colonnaded area is reminiscent of Bofill's cellar for Lafite-Rothschild (see p.51), although at Salentein the central space does have a protagonist: the stone floor is inlaid with the design of a compass signalling the four cardinal points. The stone is naturally coloured local sandstone and schist. Architects Eliana Bórmida and Mario Yanzón created the design in homage to local Andean and Inca cultures, whose skilled use of stone in their favoured mountainous regions was prodigious. "The richness we have in rock is marvellous," grins Yanzón; "we wanted to capture that."

On a practical level, the wine flows by force of gravity from the top fermentation level to the underground ageing cellars. But, thanks to the architects' imagination, the progression from overground to underground at Salentein goes beyond practicality and becomes a kind of descent into history, burrowing through cultural strata to arrive at an oddly comforting, elemental level. Bórmida describes the cellar as celebrating Pachamama, the Andean earth goddess, in "the entrails of the earth".

Juan Alcorta SPAIN

In the introduction, I quoted a producer who talked of the timeless quality that wine cellars can have. To the sceptic, this may sound fanciful. All I can do is urge you to experience it for yourself. Somewhere like Jarvis would be a good place to start. Underground spaces can have a dislocating effect on the mind. When you enter, you feel cautious and disoriented; by the time you emerge, the outside world feels alien, its smells and sounds familiar but foreign. That experience is what Jarvis is all about. It starts the moment you walk up the drive to be met by nothing more than a door in the hillside.

Jarvis is located high above California's Napa Valley in the Vacas Mountains. And it really *is* in the mountains, tunnelled in two concentric circles with intersecting diagonals and, at one end, a chamber big enough to fit a basketball court. Fibre-optic chandeliers, Brazilian granite sinks, a waterfall, and man-sized chunks of amethyst are notable features.

SOUNDS OF THE UNDERGROUND

62 WINERIES WITH STYLE

Salentein ARGENTINA >>59–60

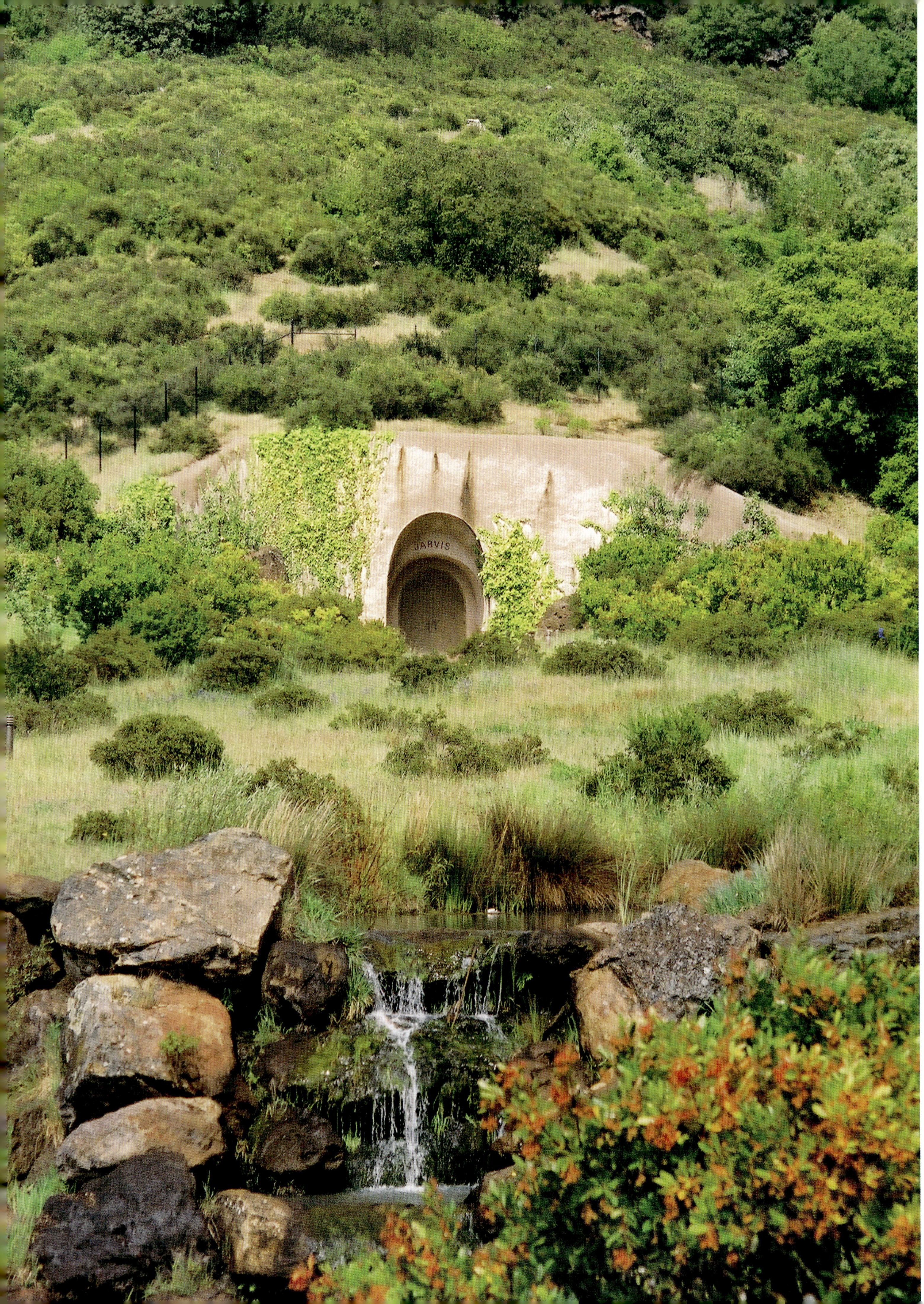
JARVIS

It's the offices, labs, and winemaking that stop you writing the place off as a subterranean sideshow. All Jarvis's wine is made and matured in these tunnels; an efficient air circulation system is critical to remove potentially lethal carbon dioxide from fermentation. Even the mini-waterfall, itself a chance discovery during excavation, adds welcome humidity to the winemaking atmosphere.

Never has underground winery design been taken to such lengths, or treated with such theatrical zeal. The experience belongs to a different plane. The day I visited, I was lucky enough to catch elusive winemaker Dmitri Tchelistcheff. We tasted in the Crystal Chamber, swilling Chardonnay and Cabernet in super-size glasses to the sound of *zarzuela* tunes. Dressed head to toe in denim, Dmitri balanced two glasses of his top Cabernet on either knee, like an indulgent grandparent. Occasionally, he grinned sheepishly or, rarer still, uttered an almost inaudible sentence. Mostly he just looked contented.

When we finally emerged from the door in the hill, it had rained. It was a hot day and steam rose from the road. The scent of bay leaves and moist grass was overpowering, the sun dazzling. I remembered a phrase I had read in Jarvis's promotional material: "Upon entering the cave, these grapes will not see the light of day again until they are sold as wine."

SOUNDS OF THE UNDERGROUND

IN BRIEF

DOMECQ LA MEZQUITA
Jerez, Spain
BUILT 1970 by Javier Soto López Doriga
WINE TIP Rio Viejo Oloroso
VISITS By appointment
www.domecq.es
Domecq's famous La Mezquita (mosque) bodega contains 4,400 arches and if you walked all its aisles, you'd travel six kilometres (three-and-a-half miles). Owned by Allied Domecq but family-controlled, and still producing fantastic sherry.

POMMERY
Champagne, France
BUILT 1868 onwards by Gosset and Gozier
WINE TIP Cuvée Louise
VISITS Open doors
www.pommery.com
From funky bottles of POP (you need a straw) to the classy Cuvée Louise, Pommery is a versatile beast with captivating cellars. Fingers crossed, the recent change in ownership will not see things go downhill.

TERRA-VINEA
Corbières, France
CONVERTED 1992
WINE TIP Grande Réserve
VISITS Open doors
www.terra-vinea.com
Terra-Vinéa is the creation of the cooperative cellar, Caves Rocbère. After the local gypsum mine was closed, Rocbère took control and converted it into a wine cellar and tourist attraction. The term terroir takes on new meaning after this trip underground.

CHATEAU AUSONE
St-Emilion, Bordeaux, France
BUILT 1524
WINE TIP Ausone 1995
VISITS By appointment
www.chateau-ausone.com
Ausone is one of the brightest stars in St-Emilion and Bordeaux. A magnificent location for both cellars and vineyards means a tiny production of usually superlative quality. Ardent owner Alain Vauthier brings the property to life.

REDI
Montepulciano, Tuscany, Italy
BUILT 1562 by Baldassare Peruzzi
WINE TIP Briareo Vino Nobile di Montepulciano
VISITS By appointment
www.cantinadelredi.com
A gem of an Italian Renaissance palazzo with cellars to match, Redi is a proud exponent of Montepulciano wine. Its enigmatic Renaissance motto "*Argo et Non Briareo*" translates as "Look but Don't Touch".

MASTROBERARDINO
Campania, Italy
BUILT 1700 onwards
WINE TIP Radici Fiano di Avellino
VISITS By appointment
www.mastroberardino.it
Located near Pompeii, Mastroberardino's passion is rescuing ancient grape varieties that have been misplaced in the mists of time. The gorgeous Fiano is one history lesson that should not be skipped, the Taurasi another. Delicious.

GONZALEZ-BYASS
Jerez, Spain
BODEGAS BUILT 1862 Gustave Eiffel; 1974 J A Torroja Cavanillas
WINE TIP Tío Pepe
VISITS Open doors
www.gonzalezbyass.es
Among the oldest and finest purveyors of sherry, González-Byass continues to move with the times. You think sherry's dull? Have a go at the excellent new-look Tío Pepe. Failing that, visit the winery.

CHATEAU LAFITE-ROTHSCHILD
Pauillac, Bordeaux, France
CELLAR BUILT 1987 by Ricardo Bofill
WINE TIP Les Carruades 1997
VISITS By appointment
www.lafite.com

In addition to boasting a celebrity cellar, Lafite produces one of Bordeaux's very finest reds. If you can't afford the top wine then Les Carruades offers a glimpse of the action from cheap(er) seats.

RAIMAT
Costers del Segre, Catalonia, Spain
BODEGAS BUILT 1918 by Rubio i Bellver; 1988 Domingo Triay
WINE TIP Raimat Abadía
VISITS By appointment
www.raimat.com

A vast estate founded in 1914 by Codorníu and now making wines in an international style. It's worth the trip just to see the two astonishing winery buildings.

CODORNIU
Penedès, Catalonia, Spain
BUILT 1915 by Josep Puig i Cadafalch
WINE TIP Cuvée Raventós
VISITS Open doors
www.codorniu.com

How refreshing to see a huge producer (the many miles of cellar hold a fair amount of wine) continuing to produce quality at all levels. The pioneering spirit is captured in the architecture – it's now a national monument.

ARTESA
Carneros, Napa, USA
BUILT 1991 by Triay/Bouligny
WINE TIP Artesa Pinot Noir
VISITS Open doors
www.artesawinery.com

Formerly known as Codorníu Napa, a quick about-turn saw this startling underground facility switch allegiances from fizz to still wine. Its location, in the cool Carneros hills, is ideal for elegant, restrained styles of wine.

JUAN ALCORTA
Rioja, Spain
BUILT 2001 by Ignacio Quemada
WINE TIP Marqués de Villamagna Gran Reserva
VISITS By appointment
www.byb.es

Alcorta is owned by the same firm as futuristic Ysios (see p.165–6) but belongs to another world. From this mammoth underground wine factory emerge reliable and readily available wines such as Campo Viejo.

SALENTEIN
Uco Valley, Mendoza, Argentina
BUILT 1999 by Bórmida & Yanzón
WINE TIP Primus Pinot Noir
VISITS Open doors
www.bodegasalentein.com

High even by Argentina's lofty standards, the Alto Uco Valley is a hugely promising winegrowing area with vineyards up to 1,700 metres (5,577 feet). Salentein is busy putting it on the map.

JARVIS
Napa Valley, USA
BUILT 1992 by William Jarvis
WINE TIP Cave-Fermented Reserve Cabernet Sauvignon
VISITS By appointment
www.jarviswines.com

"Cave-Fermented" is not a term you'll come across often on a wine label. But then, Jarvis isn't your everyday wine producer. Razzmatazz aside, the wines are very impressive and correspondingly expensive.

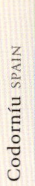

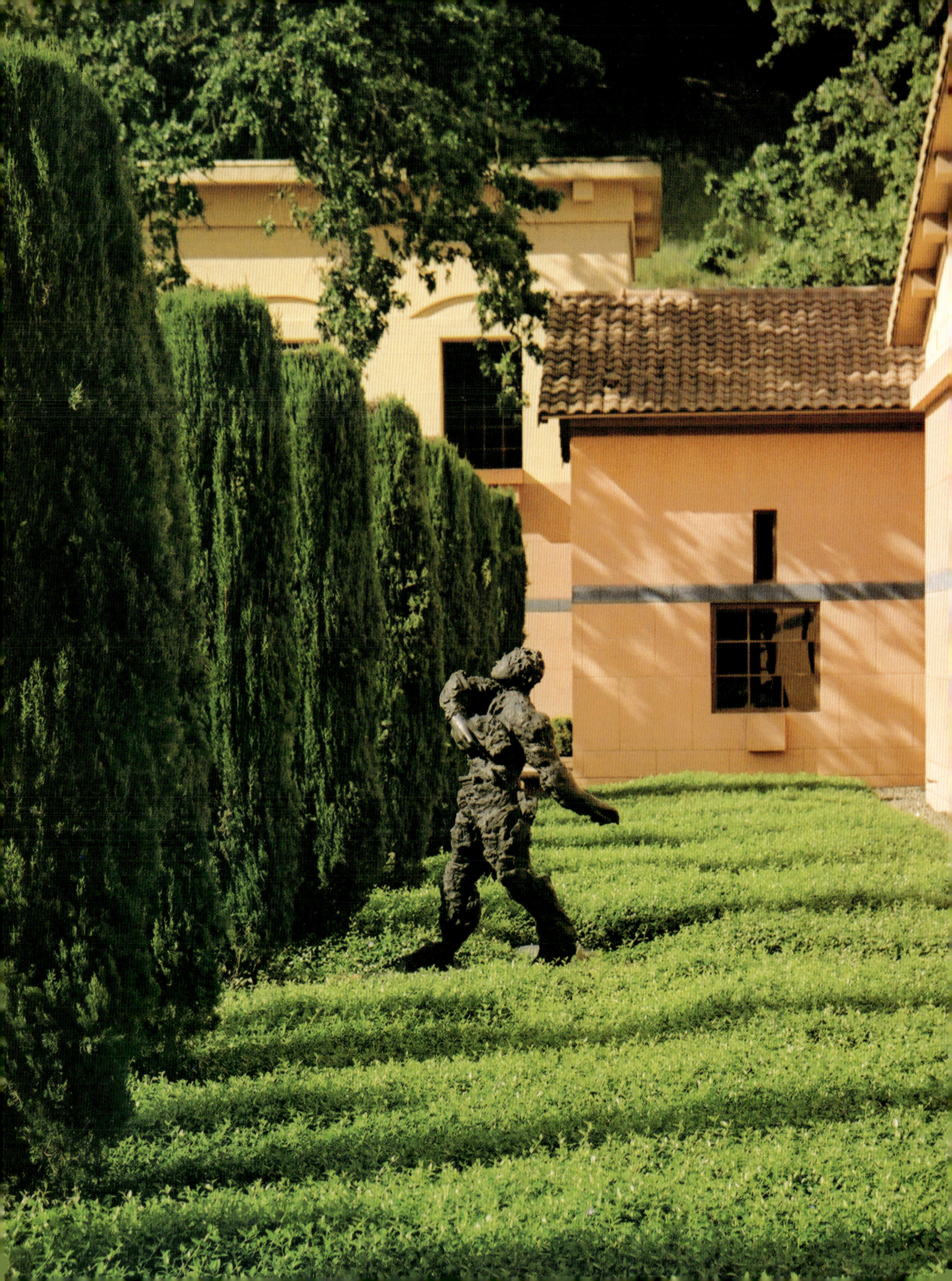

A BREATH OF FRESH AIR

BREATHING NEW LIFE INTO TRADITIONAL SURROUNDINGS

Renovation is a tricky business. It means making things new again – in this case a wine world built on decidedly traditional foundations. Wine, though, has always been about a respect for the past, but a furtive allegiance to the future. Bacchus is not just the god of wine – he also represents rebirth.

Clos Pegase USA >>71, 75

Jan Shrem makes the chair seem big. Dressed in limp grey, he talks of his life in unhurried, deliberate tones. How he wanted to be an architect but "flunked math". The publishing and property business in Japan. A passion for wine and art. By the time he comes on to talking of the competition, he seems distracted, perhaps weary, and mentions it only in the briefest of terms.

I press him. Tell me about the competition, I say – it's why I'm here. He looks startled, in the manner of a child who has been unfairly reprimanded. I try to move the conversation on, complimenting him on his art collection, office, winery. He interrupts me.

"There was opposition to the winery," he says, quietly. "They said it would look like an atomic waste disposal site, but, of course," chuckling now, intelligent eyes, I await his refutation, "they never have come up with a way to dispose of atomic waste properly, have they?"

For all his shrinking demeanour, Jan Shrem is a key figure in the emergence of the icon winery in modern times. It sounds childish to point and say, "he started

Clos Pegase USA

it", but that, effectively, is what Shrem did in 1984 when he announced an architectural competition, in conjunction with the San Francisco Museum of Modern Art, to design and build a new winery he and his wife Mitsuko wanted to name after Pegasus, the mythical winged horse. It signalled the start of the modern age of winery design.

Of course, there had been ambitious modern architectural statements in wineries before this – Shrem's immediate neighbour Sterling (*see* p.123–5) is one. Another is Mondavi (also in Napa Valley, and the founder of which, Robert Mondavi, was one of the competition's judges). But it was Shrem's astute decision to run the competition – a calculated wager, certainly not without its risks – that proved defining. Not only did it result in the sort of ground-breaking design he was after for his own winery; more importantly it set the scene for a far wider architectural resurgence in the wine world.

Nearly 100 architectural firms rose to the challenge, which was a unique one. The brief was for an artist and architect to work together in designing

A BREATH OF FRESH AIR   71

Clos Pegase USA

72 WINERIES WITH STYLE

Château Pichon-Longueville Baron FRANCE >>75–6

A BREATH OF FRESH AIR

Château Pichon-Longueville Baron FRANCE

74 WINERIES WITH STYLE

a facility that would integrate art into the process of winemaking (the Shrems are avid art collectors; Pegasus is the subject of an 1890 painting by Odilon Redon).

Architect Michael Graves ended up winning the competition, but the unsuccessful parties were perhaps just as notable. Shortly after the competition, Ricardo Bofill built Lafite-Rothschild's innovative new cellar in Bordeaux (*see* p.51). Patrick Dillon, who worked with Bofill on the Clos Pegase project, teamed up with French architect Jean de Gastines and together they went on to work on ambitious projects at Pichon-Longueville Baron, also in Bordeaux (*see* below), and South Africa's Vergelegen (*see* p.177).

The Clos Pegase competition was a landmark in its own right. Like the buildings it would ultimately help create, it was a talking point, a platform from which wine could reach a wider audience. The New World was making its mark. Respected architect Jean Dethier, in the book that accompanied the Châteaux Bordeaux Wine and Architecture Exhibition of 1988, talked of how "château hospitality has been modernized and made more democratic by the Americans."

Graves had created in Clos Pegase a showpiece winery that took classical European features and expressed them in a visitor-friendly, post-modern American arrangement. Interestingly, plans in the original design for an art museum had to be shelved owing to local legislation restricting non-agricultural developments – so the art simply became part of the furniture. Wine, art, and architecture had come together as part of one big organic spectacle. Graves later went on to work extensively for Disney.

But the architecture of wineries was not the only thing in the process of being democratized at this time – so was wine. The New World, and California in particular, was starting to rattle the likes of Bordeaux and Burgundy with the quality (and quantity) of its wine. Blind tastings in the late 1970s had already established that even professional tasters rated Californian wines just as highly as their French counterparts. Now, the wineries themselves were laying down the challenge.

The Châteaux Bordeaux Exhibition was an admirable attempt to stir the Bordelais into action in the face of such constructive provocation. Bofill's cellar at Château Lafite-Rothschild had been built a year earlier and was looking like it might just prove the start of something. Amid his exhortations, Dethier praised Clos Pegase for its "essential contribution to the renaissance of viticultural architecture", noting how "it creates a strong brand image based on architecture and theatrical effect". Bordeaux, he warned, needed to remedy its "cultural amnesia".

Château Pichon-Longueville Baron FRANCE

These were the rumblings of a revival. The most conspicuous outcome in Bordeaux was Pichon-Longueville Baron's commissioning of Dillon and de Gastines in 1988 to completely re-do its ramshackle winemaking facilities in Pauillac. It followed another, less publicized, competition and the winning design was a perfect riposte to Dethier's charge of cultural negligence. The architects still managed to have fun.

For Clos Pegase, Michael Graves had Americanized a classical European heritage. In Pichon, Dillon and de Gastines had to tread gingerly around tradition while expressing a modern vision. This being Bordeaux, there was the château to contend with – on this occasion the estate's centrepiece, one of the turreted fairytale type, built in 1851. A balance would have to be struck.

The result is a play-off between a stern exterior and ebullient interior. Outside, everything is kept subdued and subservient to the château. The new buildings crouch low to the ground, rising only as high as the château's base – even a slight incline in the winery façade mimics the senior structure. Rare architectural flourishes are minimalist motifs reprised from the château itself and the local landscape, albeit with a slight tongue in cheek, hinting at a less severe interior.

Inside, the mood changes. A circular vinification chamber with alarmingly tilted columns and a

A BREATH OF FRESH AIR

pyramidal skylight paint a very different picture. Brightly coloured geometric patterns cover the floor. Even cellarmaster Jean-René Matignon, not normally given to flights of fancy, talks of an "energy concentration" at the heart of the building. This is a vivid celebration of winemaking, all the pent-up aristocratic ardour unleashed, spilling over in what the architects term a ritualistic and theatrical spirit. It's quite some progression between old and new, but the transition is handled seamlessly and the impression is captivating.

The balance between tradition and modernity is always a tricky tightrope to walk where wine is concerned. Especially in regions like Bordeaux, where innovation inevitably meets the weight of generations and the implacable retort: "but it's always been done that way". On the one hand, Bordeaux's tradition, châteaux, experience, and knowledge of the land are

Château d'Arsac FRANCE >>77, 79–80

what make it unique and greatly prized by wine lovers. On the other, modern consumers have modern tastes and new technology cannot be ignored. Wine, inevitably, adapts.

The ideal is that the synthesis of modernity and tradition means a better glass of wine. Such a commitment to moving with the times can also be reflected in the architecture, especially in times of confidence and prosperity, as the 1980s were in Bordeaux. Pichon managed both after new owners AXA-Millésimes, a branch of the French insurers, took over in the late 1980s; a similar change of ownership and revitalisation has taken place at Château d'Arsac, a few miles away in the appellation of Margaux.

Alain Vauthier at Château Ausone (*see* p.47) put it well when he said to me, "In Bordeaux, to get a reaction, you need a crisis". In 1986, d'Arsac was floundering, a tattered remnant of a proud history stretching back to the twelfth

Château d'Arsac FRANCE

A BREATH OF FRESH AIR

Hess Collection USA >>80

78 WINERIES WITH STYLE

century. Enter new owner Philippe Raoux, who wanted to retain the architectural ensemble but invest it with a new sense of vigour and commercial identity. He hired architect Patrick Hernandez.

The word "renaissance" somehow seems wrong to describe what's taken place at d'Arsac. Rebirth can imply starting again from scratch. This was more of a resurrection. Many new vineyards were planted on the property at that time, it is true, but d'Arsac's lack of vinous prestige (unlike, say, Pichon) meant that if it was to shake off its ignominious abandon it would have to use every asset at its disposal. That meant the nineteenth century château and winery were due for a makeover.

Shocking blue may be familiar to fans of St Petersburg's monuments but it is not a colour that adorns the façades of many *cuviers* in Bordeaux. Which is probably exactly why Hernandez went with it. Classic ochre lines were retained amid the blue, but stainless steel went across the windows and old wooden doors. "The idea," I was told, "is that entering the *cuvier* should be like entering a winemaking tank." The overall impression is bold, almost aggressive.

But d'Arsac isn't just about a simple shock and awe exercise. What makes it compelling is the way you think you've got it covered and then it surprises you. Take the château. By day, it looks a normal, fairly sedate affair beside its prim lake. But inside, it's a revelation in interior design, with a marked Japanese feel to its lightness and strength. The effect is crowned by the central roof, which is in fact made more of glass than tiles, and which night-time lights illuminate like a beacon that can be seen for some distance.

This is Dethier's democratic château: a former manor house that's had the stuffing ripped out and a bonfire of frivolity lit inside with its remnants. D'Arsac is a place to be visited, enjoyed, and discussed. Modern artworks litter the property in a manner reminiscent of Clos Pegase. And for all this, the estate still retains a sense of history, both in its architecture and in its wines, the latter of which remain faithful to the time-honoured appellation of Margaux. Raoux even has his château to put on the label.

The breath of fresh air scouring the wine world has not just inspired architectural renovation, but also artistic endeavour. As wine has started to shed its elitist image and wineries become destinations for more than just the committed wine devotee, the more welcoming of wineries have pondered the concept of synergy. How to stand out from the crowd? Architecture is one answer, art another. The result is something akin to a cultural superstore – everything under one roof.

Clos Pegase and Château d'Arsac are by no means the only contenders. One other winery stirring up a fine blend of wine, art, and architecture is the Hess Collection, high in Napa Valley's Mount Veeder. What is rare here is that the winery-cum-gallery wasn't built from scratch, as many New World wineries tend to be. This time American, not French, history had to be courted.

Two stone buildings dating back to 1903 (a three-storey winery and single-storey distillery) came with the territory when Swiss magnate Donald Hess acquired it in 1986. Loath to destroy such heritage, Hess's brief included retaining the original structures but developing the site to house modern winemaking facilities and a gallery for his art collection. The task of realizing this somewhat eclectic vision fell to Swiss architect Beat Jordi.

Wandering around the airy two-floor art gallery now, mulling over the odd piece of modern art, it's easy to forget what these buildings once were. It's only in the reception lobby, where the two ends of each stone structure have been intelligently left bare, that you can get a sense of the conversion work that has been carried out here. History has been retained and modernity injected. The architectural report was more modest, simply saying "when other building elements were added, the stone walls fortunately remained intact".

The real masterstroke at Hess is the way in which the winemaking has been brought into the arena of the art gallery. At one point, a colossal female portrait by Franz Gertsch, startling in its almost photographic clarity, hangs next to a tinted window that looks onto the winery's bottling line. The banalities of the winemaking process are transformed into art by association. A few steps away, a deep-set gable window makes the perfect frame for a view over an old vineyard combing the crest of a hill. You start to wonder what's art and what's not.

The experience is, if nothing else, novel. Seldom have wine, art, and architecture been so integrated as they are at Hess, disciplines converging in almost disorienting fashion. Was this a uniquely American inspiration? Hardly – Château Mouton-Rothschild, for one, had been doing something similar in Bordeaux since the 1960s. But, like the Romans with plumbing, the Americans can be credited with making it mainstream.

For all the fervent and ultimately positive rivalry between the Americans and French, however, another nation bears a large responsibility for taking the modern architecture of wine beyond its traditional horizons: Spain. Its architects and wine producers, both in Spain and abroad, have been nothing short of pioneering. Rafael Moneo's construction at Chivite's Señorío de Arínzano estate in Navarra is an object lesson in how sensitivity to the environment and the past can still leave room for original creation.

Arínzano offered Moneo a similar challenge to the one that Dillon and de Gastines had faced at Pichon-Longueville (*see* p.75) – how to insert a functional, industrial facility into a tricky natural and historic environment. In this case, nature in the form of the River Ega and the surrounding tree populations, and history in the form of a tightly knit but motley collection of three old buildings: a sixteenth century tower, a neoclassical chapel, and an eighteenth century manor house.

One of Moneo's key works prior to Arínzano had been his museum of Roman art in Mérida. It is an exceptional building, in which Moneo manages to evoke a very classical Roman atmosphere in bricks and high arches, but also to convey a thoroughly modern feel. That delicate effect of reflecting history while making a modern statement is what he reproduces in a somewhat different format at Arínzano.

The modern winery gently frames the old buildings on three sides, its exterior unobtrusive and complementary. As with Pichon, the interior comes alive, although Moneo's style is more sober and subtle. Light falls in quirky geometric patterns from sparse skylights. Views out through tinted windows plant the gravitational centre of the winery firmly among the historic edifices. The winery's one grandiose statement is found in the barrel cellar, the winemaking equivalent of the hall of Valhalla, where huge V-shaped timber beams converge for hundreds of feet around a raised walkway. It is, in effect, the winery's backbone.

Badia a Coltibuono ITALY >>82

A BREATH OF FRESH AIR

Crates of green-gold Chardonnay grapes were being unloaded and diligently sorted the day I arrived. Frenetic activity rarely surrounds wine, save for the first few days of its existence. The scene, from the busy workers to the winery and the antique buildings beyond, was a poignant expression of living history. No doubt it was as Moneo intended.

The challenge of breathing new life into historical wine estates has produced many diverse architectural solutions in recent times. Pichon-Longueville, d'Arsac, Hess, and Chivite are all examples of imaginative close-quarters modernization. When a new winery was planned for the historic Badia a Coltibuono wine estate in the Tuscan hills of Chianti, the architects had relative space to work with by comparison, although the result is just as ingenious.

Few regions can match the way Chianti captures the spirit of fine country life in its wine, architecture, landscape, and people. The sense of history can be overwhelming. The imposing abbey (*badia*) of Coltibuono was established by Benedictines in the eleventh century. The new winery, though a ten-minute drive from the abbey, would have to reflect this environment and yet still give the impression of modernity.

There is something of the Moneo touch about Piero Sartogo and Nathalie Grenon's winery. It's respectful and subtle, but still contemporary. Clever skylights and scattered buttonhole windows give the exterior a dynamic appeal, and create soft lighting inside. The volume of the building, which is appreciable, is broken up by the juxtaposition of cylindrical structures, diagonal lines, and raised brickwork. It's one of those buildings which, when caught out of the corner of the eye, could either be medieval or modern. It has the dimensions of a castle or defensive rampart, of which no shortage exists in Tuscany.

The structure is cleverly worked into its wooded environment, like Arínzano, and also the side of a hill, like Hess, to allow grapes and wine to flow through the winemaking process by gravity (the total drop is around thirteen metres, or forty-three feet). The diagonal paths that break up the winery's façade echo the paths that climb from the winery up the hill behind. Since 2000, the estate has been working on an organic programme – a process they describe in terms that could be a description of the winery: "rediscovering traditional techniques and integrating them with modern scientific understanding".

For all the seriousness, though, you get the feeling that there's a little bit of fun being had at history's

Schloss Wackerbarth GERMANY >>85–6

expense. A slight cheekiness in the design that brings the whole thing to life. If it's a feature that hovers just below the surface at Coltibuono, it's most definitely out in the open at Loimer.

Fred Loimer is a fiercely committed Austrian winegrower and champion of his native Kamp Valley (Kamptal). When he bought the large Haindorf Castle cellar outside the city of Langenlois in 1999, the press house was beyond repair. New buildings were needed. "To imitate an ancient style was out of the question," says Loimer. "I chose contemporary architecture to match with the plain, yet fantastic cellar." Plain could be considered an understatement for what resulted.

Severely minimalist is a more accurate way of describing the stark concrete interiors and angular matt black exterior of the new building, which houses offices and tasting rooms above the cellar. Architect Andreas Burghardt worked toward a "strict geometry", like a cube. The shape of the building above ground is intended to echo the nineteenth-century cellar below, as is the interior design (bare walls, corridor-like spaces.) Loimer claims he had felt stifled in Langenlois. His reaction to life at the new buildings makes him sound like a monk with a new monastery. "It's incredibly quiet here. I enjoy the purism, the breath of freedom. And there is a feeling of composure, which is terribly good for the soul."

There's something of the endearingly childlike about Loimer's enthusiasm and desire to challenge preconceptions. In a wine sense, it's very healthy – he describes himself as "eager to try new things". His words apply just as much to the architecture of his new building as it does to his wine. It does seem faintly ironic that with his futuristic new wine architecture, Fred Loimer is a fully paid-up member of the Austrian Association of Traditional Wineries. This probably refers less to the winery than to the style of his wines, which aim to express the character of the land, just as generations have before.

Schloss Wackerbarth GERMANY

A BREATH OF FRESH AIR

VINOS
VINOS
R. LOPEZ DE HEREDIA
VIÑA TONDONIA, S.A.
R. LOPEZ DE HEREDIA
VIÑA TONDONIA. S.A.

López de Heredia SPAIN

Sometimes, it is refreshing to see things stripped down to bare bones. Especially in an industry like wine, where it's all too easy to get lost amid all the wines, regions, vintages, and producers, not to mention all the posturing and flowery language. In this sense, it's heartening to see an architectural trend towards transparency emerging in wine, which not only helps bring the subject to people in an approachable fashion but also encourages rigorous production among producers.

But what if the posturing and transparency are combined in wine architecture? Most stylish wineries have an element of attention-seeking about them, from Margaux (*see* p.20) to Mezzacorona (*see* p.177), so to open the winemaking process up within such an environment makes for compelling viewing. A good example of how such openness can revive a traditional domain is Schloss Wackerbarth, which needs to grab all the attention it can due to its isolated location in Saxony, eastern Germany. "It's Germany's smallest and most unknown region," says Wackerbarth's Jörg Christöphler, plaintively.

Adversity tends to foster creativity, though, and you get the impression at Wackerbarth that sitting idly to await an anonymous fate is not an option

A BREATH OF FRESH AIR 85

(Christöphler at one point has to stop himself and apologize for his "self-addicted characterization"). The *schloss* itself is a respectable eighteenth century manor house with impeccable Teutonic trimmings – manicured lawns and trees surround the house and outbuildings in faultless symmetry. In fact, the sense of order is almost too perfect, so to see the dominion of nature assert itself in steep terraced vineyards above a dinky belvedere is refreshing. A similar breath of fresh air comes in the form of the new winery.

In contrast to the contrived baroque sensibilities of the old buildings and gardens, Wackerbarth's new winery is unassuming. The relatively simple structure is made from stone, steel, wood, and glass. Inside, the building is spacious and well lit, the winemaking process presented for all to see. A glass façade gives views out onto the older parts and the vineyard, but is protected from direct sunlight by horizontal wooden slats (a much-used design feature in wine, allowing light in but protecting against heat). The spectacle is not the winery itself but everything around it and inside it.

Christöphler talks admirably of how "architecture should reflect the style of the period it's built in". In this case, it's 1730s baroque meets twenty-first century modernity. One criticism is that the winery is hardly well integrated into the overall design of the property, but that's also its charm. It breaks up the order but in a subtle way that draws attention, not to itself, but to the winemaking process. Both architectural styles faithfully reflect attitudes toward building and the environment of their times.

On the belvedere at Wackerbarth is the inscription "Generations are passing by like clouds past the sun". If you filter out the baroque melodrama, you can almost hear the architecture critic John Ruskin's comment about walls that are "long washed by the passing waves of humanity". Architecture that moves and modernizes with the times inevitably incorporates elements that can at first seem disparate or discordant, but that is, in a sense, the point. Even architectural master Antoni Gaudí, who was obsessed by his masterpiece, the Sagrada Familia cathedral in Barcelona, said he would rather not finish the building in his lifetime because architectural work should be the fruit of a long era. He died, run over by a tram, in 1926, and work has continued.

Architectural work in progress is a defining feature of the López de Heredia winery in Rioja. "The original architectural project started in 1877," María López de Heredia told me, "and it's been ongoing ever since." The winery has an impeccable

Hermann J. Wiemer USA >>87

reputation as a producer of classic style Rioja wines, aged and age-worthy. An eclectic, sprawling nineteenth century architecture is its hallmark. Progress, however, means constant innovation and the current generation of family owners also look set to add their own layer of history to the property.

The family commissioned the avant-garde firm of Zaha Hadid to produce a unique piece of architectural design. "It's a new pavilion to contain an older pavilion," explains project architect Jim Heverin. "The old pavilion had been found in their outhouses and restored to its original condition. It had been originally commissioned by the great-grandfather for the World Fair exhibition in 1910." The idea is that revamping the old timber pavilion will prove the start of a whole new wave of modern architecture at López de Heredia – a sort of Russian doll effect, in Heverin's words.

Despite being placed firmly in a wider context of regeneration, it's hard to overlook the new structure. Hadid is well known for her bold and innovative designs, creating strange and surprising spaces by complex geometrical interplay, and this pavilion looks to be no different. "For us the starting point was to jump into the future to determine how the present would evolve," says Heverin. Pondering the issue led the architects to develop a rectangular housing for the old pavilion, which then morphs into a shape reminiscent of a decanter. "We had designed a new bottle for an old wine," is their verdict.

The Russian doll style of revival has also been employed at Hermann J. Wiemer's winery in the Finger Lakes region of New York State. This time, however, the structure in need of a refit was an unsuspecting barn, and the solution quite different from that at López de Heredia.

Although he was talking about his own winery, Fred Loimer (*see* p.83) could have been describing Wiemer's barn when he said: "the building is like a bottle of wine: initially closed-in, simple, and plain from the outside; but when you open it, a wonderful world opens up before you." From the outside, this is nothing more than a dark barn whose size is emphasized by the many small windows on its south wall. Inside, however, the architects have inserted a towering white structure with four white legs like classical columns. Delicate light filters in through the small windows. The barn is now a fully working winery and ageing facility for sparkling wine. Wiemer was so impressed by the conversion that he initially lived in the new building (as Fred Loimer has at his).

"It's pretty unique, with lots of character," Wiemer says of his barn winery. "It's great for cold stabilization in the winter; it can get to minus ten around here, but I don't think it would work in warmer California," he says with a smile. Wiemer is no stranger to cool climates; he was born in Germany's Mosel winelands. According to critic Susan Doubilet, the architects wanted to play on the notion of Wiemer being in the USA but not of it – hence the striking interplay between the new structure and its old barn surroundings. The confluence of cultures in the area is echoed in local town names like Dundee, Ovid, Geneva, and Waterloo.

Population movements around the world have given rise to many new architectural phenomena throughout history. One example is Cape Dutch in South Africa, a style inspired by Amsterdam

Hermann J. Wiemer USA

A BREATH OF FRESH AIR 87

merchant houses but adapted over time to reflect South African realities. The typical picture today of Cape Dutch is clean, whitewashed walls, thatched roofs, and gables like proud figureheads – one of the classic images of the Cape and its winelands.

The Rustenberg estate near Stellenbosch has a winemaking tradition and buildings that date back to the seventeenth century. Subsequent building over the years retained the historic, tightly knit appeal of the Cape Dutch estate, so when owner Simon Barlow came to expand production by sixty per cent, he wanted a winery that would fit into the historic and natural context, yet still deliver on the winemaking front.

"Ach, just take a dairy, kick out the cows and shove in the wine stuff." Such is winemaker Adi Badenhorst's no-nonsense verdict on how it was done. In reality, architect Simon Beerstecher faced an intricate challenge and overcame it in style. He did indeed use the old dairy shed, retaining the thick walls, timber thatch roof, and main gable (the cows, a prize Jersey herd, now occupy new facilities nearby). Not only that, but the old stable and seventeenth century barn were also to be brought up to scratch, for a tasting room and bottling line, respectively. This was no simple conversion job.

One of Château Margaux's (*see* p.20) most vaunted features is the sense of unity in the whole collection of estate buildings; Rustenberg has

Rustenberg SOUTH AFRICA >>88, 90

A BREATH OF FRESH AIR

similar qualities. Beerstecher simply retained that balance. His solution was to build the bulk of the new winery underground, using the hillside to maximum effect, while squeezing every inch out of the new and old buildings above ground. Steel trusses were fitted under thatched roofs to house suspended stainless-steel tanks, leaving the floor space free for work. A glass-walled conference room was inserted over the barrel cellar. Four bristling levels of winemaking are neatly packed into the unassuming, whitewashed old cowshed.

Both architect and owner talk of "layers of history" in the architecture. The overall result is a subtle, graceful impression, not only of an efficient working environment, but also of a powerful sense of place. Amid the distant moos and soothing smell of dried grass thatch, I turn to take my leave. As I do so, I catch sight of winemaker Adi. I notice his boots, which have worn down to the steel toe-cap. "That's from kicking all the cows, " he quips as he disappears into the former cowshed.

"Layers of history" is an evocative phrase. Not only is it a nod to the importance of the past, it also recognizes that modern input is a fundamental part of the process. What we might consider futuristic today could become tomorrow's tradition. In this chapter, we have seen how individual wine producers have approached this process of modernization, but it can be a collective occurrence, too.

Beside the Goulburn River in Victoria, Australia, stand two towers. One belongs to Tahbilk – a stately, antique affair – while the other rises fifty-five metres (180 feet) above the Mitchelton winery in a declamatory, modern manner. They could not be more different in style, and yet, so close together, sharing the same riverbank, they seem generations apart, but still related.

No winery embodies winemaking history in Australia more than Tahbilk. Founded in 1860, it even took on the title Château Tahbilk for a time,

Rustenberg SOUTH AFRICA

Tahbilk AUSTRALIA >>90, 95

A BREATH OF FRESH AIR

Tahbilk AUSTRALIA

92 WINERIES WITH STYLE

Mitchelton AUSTRALIA ≫90, 95

A BREATH OF FRESH AIR

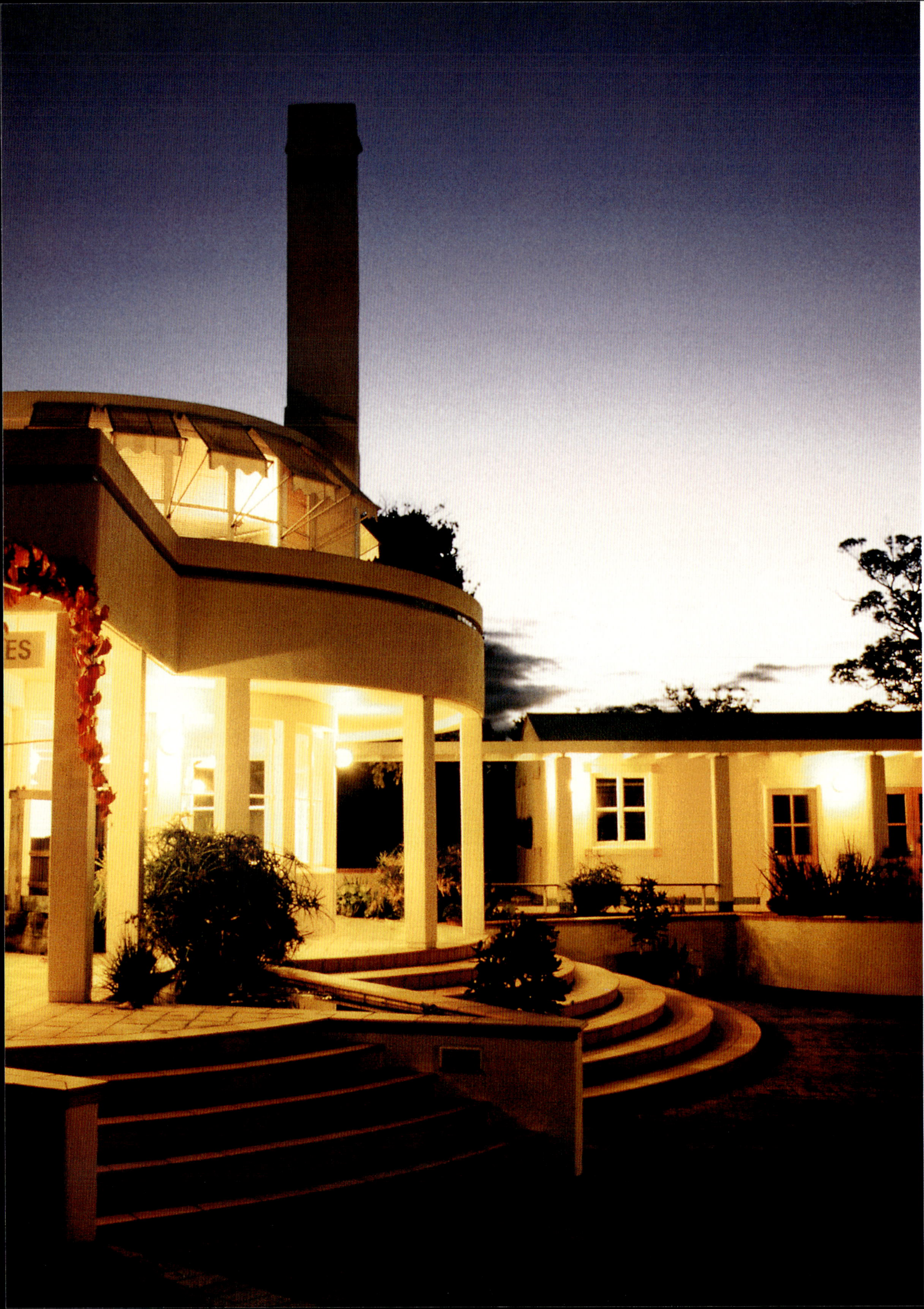

weathering many stormy times to survive as one of the oldest working wineries in the country. Its gradual evolution included building the trademark tower not long after it was founded. The then manager of the estate, François Coueslant, outlined its purpose in a letter dated July 15, 1882: the first floor was for receiving grapes at harvest; the second for storing oats; the third for keeping an eye on his vineyard workers – "which fact being known", he comments drily, "might help the work a little".

The tower today has come to symbolize Tahbilk's proud history and still adorns its labels. Owner Alister Purbick explains how "we would like to think of Tahbilk as a working museum, and that the visitors to the winery feel that they have somehow stepped back in time." The wines also reflect that history, none more so than the Shiraz made from vines originally planted in 1860. Though the winery is not short on accolades, wine writer Max Allen puts it neatly in saying: "in a country that has little sense of its own history, Tahbilk is hugely important."

Mitchelton, by contrast, flaunts its modernity. It was the first modern winery to join Tahbilk in the region and its architecture is categorical about that fact. And yet, for all their differences, both Mitchelton and Tahbilk benefit from each other's presence. Neither's architecture is particularly derivative or easily categorized; they seem to characterize the local region and little else, evidence of the constantly evolving history of winemaking along the Goulburn River.

Australia and New Zealand are generally short on striking and original architectural landmarks (the Sydney Opera House being a singular exception). All the more reason for wine, an ideal patron, to step into the breach. But how to express a sense of place and cultural identity in something akin to an architectural vacuum? Architect Ian Athfield's creations at the Te Mata wine estate in Hawke's Bay, New Zealand, are a perfect riposte.

The name Te Mata derives from local Maori language and is thought to be based on the legend of how New Zealand's North Island was wrenched up from the depths of the ocean by Maui's great fishing hook. When Athfield completed his first building at Te Mata in 1981, a house for part-owners John and Wendy Buck, it seemed he, too, had been delving into a more primeval realm. The white plastering and simple interplay of shapes are reminiscent of the most haunting, elemental North African architecture. It has an ancient feel to it, though clearly modern.

The Bucks' house, in its arresting vineyard setting, is undoubtedly one of the wine world's most enigmatic buildings, and an icon in the same sense as Château Margaux (*see* p.20). But, like Margaux,

Te Mata is more than just an impressive residence – it's part of a working, historic wine estate with one winery building (a former stable, now a barrel cellar) dating back to 1872.

Athfield has effectively given the old wine estate format a modern makeover. The basic idea is the same – an impressive estate house, winery buildings that reflect and harmonize with it, vineyards to give the whole thing meaning – but it's like a different language, a new expression that fits its contemporary New Zealand context flawlessly. "The important feature of the architecture," John Buck tells me, "is its use in creating an environment where pride in what we do is encouraged." He talks of how it "identifies us as being independent and individual, with a sense of place."

Above all, the architecture at Te Mata doesn't try too hard. Its brand of modernity reflects a typically Kiwi blend of European heritage and rugged independence. John Buck tells the story of how his passion for Hawke's Bay was initially stirred by a memorable wine from the area that, he said, displayed "the aroma that I had left behind in Europe". The scent in question was classic Bordeaux. What motivated Buck in winegrowing terms was the potential to express the special character of the land. In the architecture of Te Mata, he has the ideal landmark.

Te Mata NEW ZEALAND

A BREATH OF FRESH AIR 95

IN BRIEF

CLOS PEGASE
Napa Valley, USA
BUILT 1987 by Michael Graves
WINE TIP Hommage Cabernet Sauvignon
VISITS Open doors
www.clospegase.com
When the jury to select Clos Pegase's architect reviewed the winning entry, they praised its "celebration of Napa lifestyle". Hugely influential in design terms, less so in wine so far, though new Pinot Noirs look interesting.

CHATEAU PICHON-LONGUEVILLE BARON
Pauillac, Bordeaux, France
BUILT 1992 by Dillon and de Gastines
WINE TIP 1997 vintage
VISITS Open doors
www.chateaupichonlongueville.com
Following its purchase by AXA in the late 1980s, Pichon has undergone a revival. Wine quality has risen and a striking new winery to accompany the fairy-tale château has brought Pauillac bang up to date.

CHATEAU D'ARSAC
Margaux, Bordeaux, France
RENOVATED 1996 by Patrick Hernandez
WINE TIP 2000 vintage
VISITS By appointment
www.chateau-arsac.net
D'Arsac has been enjoying a colourful new lease of life after current owner Philippe Raoux took over in 1986, and not just in terms of the architecture. The château won the right to classify its wines as appellation Margaux in 1995

HESS COLLECTION
Mount Veeder, Napa Valley, USA
RENOVATED 1989 by Beat Jordi
WINE TIP Collection Napa Chardonnay
VISITS Open doors
www.hesscollection.com
Swiss tycoon Donald Hess has a spectacular collection of modern art and has chosen to display it in this specially adapted winery-cum-gallery. The wines made in this renovated facility, whose origins date back to 1903, are delicious.

CHIVITE SENORIO DE ARINZANO
Navarra, Spain
BUILT 2001 by Rafael Moneo
WINE TIP Colección 125 Gran Reserva Tinto
VISITS By appointment
www.chivite.es
This project was a home-coming for the Navarrese Moneo and a confirmation of Chivite's status among Spain's A-list. The winery will house production of the superb Colección 125 range.

BADIA A COLTIBUONO
Chianti, Tuscany, Italy
BUILT 1999 by Sartogo and Grenon
WINE TIP Vin Santo del Chianti Classico
VISITS Open doors
www.coltibuono.com
Coltibuono is a Chianti estate undergoing a metamorphosis, with an organic programme and new winery. Wines are somewhat indecisive as a result. Both winery and medieval *badia*, or abbey, are tourist attractions in their own right.

LOIMER
Kamptal, Austria
BUILT 2000 by Andreas Burghardt
WINE TIP Steinmassl Riesling Trocken
VISITS By appointment
www.loimer.at
If you thought black boxes belong on planes, think again. Fred Loimer's angular new winery is built above nineteenth century cellars, as austere as some of his lovingly crafted Kamptal whites.

WINERIES WITH STYLE

SCHLOSS WACKERBARTH
Saxony, Germany
BUILT 2002 by Thomas Strauch-Stoll
WINE TIP Weissburgunder Spätlese
VISITS Open doors
www.schloss-wackerbarth.de

Since reunification, Saxony is Germany's smallest wine-growing region. Wackerbarth is a big presence in the area, with an immaculate baroque manor house and brand new winery and restaurant facilities. Fascinating.

LOPEZ DE HEREDIA
Rioja, Spain
COMPLETION 2004 by Zaha Hadid
WINE TIP Viña Gravonia Crianza Blanco
VISITS By appointment
www.lopezdeheredia.com

Construction has been ongoing since 1877 at this traditional, reliably good Rioja producer. All the more reason to commend their spirit of adventure in hiring the visionary architectural firm Zaha Hadid to add a touch of pizzazz to proceedings.

HERMANN J. WIEMER
Finger Lakes, New York State, USA
BUILT 1982 by UKZ
WINE TIP Johannisberg Riesling Dry
VISITS Open doors
www.wiemer.com

Wiemer is a charismatic German émigré who shunned the hybrid vine varieties traditionally grown in this cold region and planted noble stock such as Riesling. He chose a barn for his winery and its refit has proved memorable.

RUSTENBERG
Simonsberg, Stellenbosch, South Africa
RENOVATED 1999 by Simon Beerstecher
WINE TIP John X Merriman
VISITS Open doors
www.rustenberg.co.za

A historic Cape Dutch estate that underwent a substantial refit and has emerged all guns blazing. The neat new winery was a cowshed – the prize Jersey herd has relocated. Impressively complex, age-worthy wines at the top end.

TAHBILK
Goulburn Valley, Victoria, Australia
BUILT 1860 onwards
WINE TIP 1860 vines Shiraz
VISITS Open doors
www.tahbilk.com.au

This is Australia's senior wine statesman, in its youth a witness to the mid-nineteenth century Victoria gold rush. It enjoys iconic status not just for its history and tower, but also for its wines, some of the best in the country and effortlessly world class.

MITCHELTON
Goulburn Valley, Victoria, Australia
BUILT 1974 by Robin Boyd
WINE TIP Crescent
VISITS Open doors
www.mitchelton.com.au

Mitchelton was the first winery to join Tahbilk on the Goulburn River in the modern era. The historic winery was welcoming, giving the newcomer not just cuttings to plant new vineyards but also inspiration for a soaring tower.

TE MATA
Hawke's Bay, New Zealand
BUILT 1981 onwards by John Athfield
WINE TIP Bullnose Syrah
VISITS Open doors
www.temata.co.nz

Architect Athfield has been working his magic on the estate since 1981 though the winery dates back to 1872. Te Mata has become a landmark for Hawke's Bay, for wine as well as architecture.

Rustenberg SOUTH AFRICA

Chivite Señorío de Arínzano SPAIN

López de Heredia SPAIN

A BREATH OF FRESH AIR 97

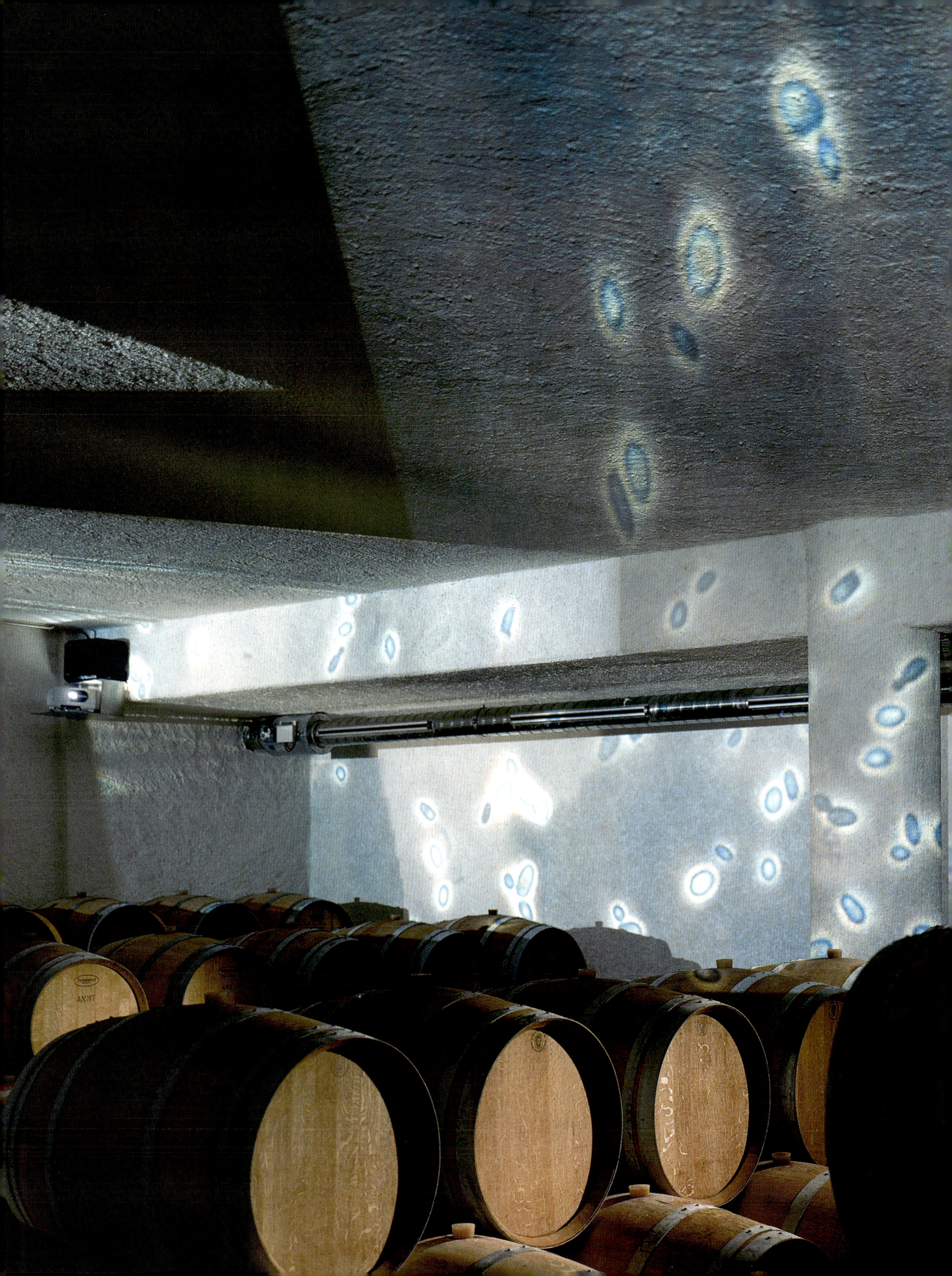

Ancient Made Modern

THE PAST GETS A
MODERN MAKEOVER

Ancient doesn't just mean old buildings. It means time-worn beliefs and local experience – a wealth of living history that is being revived to great effect. As one wine producer told me, "there's nothing new that can be invented; we just put things together in different ways". And what ways.

Alois Lageder Löwengang ITALY >>100–2

Ninna-nanna. "They did tests. They played different types of music to different glasses of water. Then they froze them. In each glass, the nature of the frozen crystals was different."

Ninna-nanna. It means lullaby. Bathed in bluish light, Alois Lageder is leaning decorously on a barrel and discussing one of the unique art installations at his Löwengang winery in Italy's mountainous northern reaches. It's Mario Airò's "Lullaby for Casks and Strings".

The setting is Lageder's petite barrel cellar. Slide projections of globular microbes in liquid (in fact, wine as seen under a microscope) are thrown in blue hues onto the walls and ceiling; it's a surreal atmosphere. And then you hear it. Long, mournful notes come and go, the sound unrecognizable but oddly familiar. Airò has stretched one minute of Bach's Sixth Brandenburg Concerto into an hour-long tape; the elongated tones only play when a wind turbine on the roof powers it.

Lageder grins broadly, a quizzical hint in his eye. When I ask if he thinks this environment affects the wine, he shrugs and talks to me of frozen water. He

Alois Lageder Löwengang ITALY

goes on, "If music can affect humans so profoundly, subconsciously as well as consciously, why not wine too? Bacteria and yeasts are living micro-organisms in wine as it matures; perhaps they feel the vibrations. The way the mechanism itself is set up means it's connecting nature to wine even as it ages – the wind is brought inside, if you like, in sound." And why Bach? "The master of harmony," smiles Alois.

Lageder is no frothing madman. He's an intelligent, pragmatic character, immensely likeable and down to earth. But the winery, like the man, is nothing short of intriguing. Not only is it fascinating in its own right, but it also captures in solid form an attitude toward wine and wineries that is not so much revolutionary as a profound rediscovery, and one which is fast gaining widespread support across the wine world. It's the holistic approach.

This attitude involves a renewed respect for nature and acceptance of its often-unexplained ways, reviving local or ancient practices, combining simple human needs with environmental balance and sustainability. It stems from an open and

ANCIENT MADE MODERN

Alois Lageder Löwengang ITALY

inquiring mind. Just as organic or biodynamic wine-growing can often be a result of this attitude in the vineyard, now the winery is being adapted to embody and incorporate the same principles.

It's the ancient made modern. As Lageder comments, "when you build new cellars, you want to capture that special atmosphere of old cellars. But you get to the point where you realize you can't just recreate. You have to look forward." Löwengang is not just a quirky mix of respect for the past and innovative design. Lageder's view is that, while the past and the environment offer immense potential for instruction, the tools and expertise of the modern era are just as important. He puts it well when he says "technology has taken us away from nature. In reality it can and should bring us closer."

The solar panels that gild the winery's angular alpine roof are one of many examples at Löwengang of harnessing technology to respect nature – the aim, when panelling is completed, is to be largely independent of the local electricity grid. Natural elements (stone, wood, sunlight) are employed to avoid what is termed "negative influences from synthetics". Nowhere is this more evident than in the offices, where natural light streams in through a central, glass-roofed atrium and onto three clear glass cubes overflowing with stone, soil, and natural vegetation. It's the work of another artist, Christian Philipp Müller, who decided to bring inside three of Lageder's vineyards, each with its unique and undamaged nature. It's all aimed at creating what is evocatively defined as "liveability".

The art at Löwengang is designed to echo the values that Lageder makes plain in the winery itself, such as sustainability and energy efficiency. What impresses is the way that the theory and practice come together in such vivid, often playful fashion. You get the feeling that Lageder doesn't take himself too seriously but is utterly committed in his endeavour.

The wine world needs its mavericks, those people who are firm enough in their convictions, however seemingly outlandish, to stir up debate and challenge preconceptions. One winery laying down such a challenge is Summerhill, where the contention runs as follows: wines matured in a pyramid taste better. We're in Canada. Overlooking the placid scenery of Lake Okanagan sits a scale replica of the Great Pyramid of Giza in Egypt. Owner Stephen Cipes is adamant: years of blind tastings have established that wines matured in the "sacred geometry" of the pyramid are consistently preferred to the same wines aged in a conventional cellar.

Cipes' argument is a fascinating one. True pyramids, he asserts, attract a unique confluence of forces that can have surprising effects. He cites experiments in replica pyramids that have shown the environment to prevent the rotting of meat, which instead petrifies, and actually to sharpen razor blades with time. Regarding wine, the Summerhill belief is that the pyramid "clarifies" liquids, highlighting flaws, as well as exaggerating qualities. "We humans are mostly made of liquid," relates the winery website, "and [we] seem to be affected by the chamber as well. We can actually feel our own 'life force energy' strengthen within the Pyramid!"

To test his theory, Cipes built a small-scale pyramid in 1989 and went on to build the larger, current version in 1997. The building was astronomically aligned to true north, as opposed to magnetic north, and no ferrous materials were used in construction, to avoid magnetic realignment (fibreglass was used instead of steel). The site was checked beforehand for underground streams, electrical sources, and gas pipelines for potential interference.

Before labelling Cipes' creation little more than an inspired piece of showmanship, it's worth bearing in mind how little we still know about the pyramids at Giza. These vast edifices exhibit a highly advanced understanding of astronomy, geometry, and mathematics in their tremendously precise and momentous construction – the "sacred geometry" to which Cipes refers. The pyramids, meanwhile, remain as inscrutable and enigmatic as the Sphinx.

And, as for how they influence what's inside, if at all – it's up for debate. Cipes' audacity at Summerhill is undoubtedly shrewd marketing, but it's also provocative, asking questions to which no easy answers exist.

The rationale behind biodynamics is dismissed by some as fanciful New Age mysticism – and perhaps it is. But if it makes the wine taste better, the environment healthier, and encourages a sense of appreciative humility towards the natural world on the part of wine producers and consumers, then the arguments start to gain weight. "I don't understand how it works, but it does, so I do it," is how winemaker Noël Pinguet of legendary French wine estate Domaine Huët defines his attitude to biodynamics. His wines bear him out and there are increasing numbers of producers like him. Biodynamics is like an extension of organic viticulture; not only are synthetic chemicals avoided, but specialist homeopathic treatments are used on the soils and plants, and particular attention paid to, not only the influence of sun, but also the stars. To some, the concept of getting up in the middle of the night to administer a dynamized solution of cow horn to the vines seems far-fetched; to producers who've seen their wines measurably improved by such practices, such objections seem petty.

Just as the pyramids seem to point to some astral significance beyond our comprehension, so biodynamics is a challenge to look beyond our accepted parameters. What is sure, though, is that in general terms it encourages a healthy focus on the vineyard and its potentially unique character, as well as a broad consideration of wine and all that surrounds and influences it. This is only to be encouraged.

Romanin in Provence is an example of a biodynamic wine producer with cellars to match. Its site, in a natural "V" on the northern side of the Alpilles ridge, has reputedly been considered sacred since prehistoric times, with Druidic and Greek cults the first evidence of such a past. The area certainly has a strong presence, with dramatic, rugged scenery and severe Mediterranean light. At Romanin they believe that their site is at a confluence of cosmic and land currents and their aim is to make wines that are "messengers of a place and a history". Biodynamics is one ingredient in that formula; the architect Serge Hennemann produced another.

Romanin's wine cellar is dug into the rock, a cavernous space with soaring arches and bare rock walls. Just as both cosmic and terrestrial forces form part of biodynamic viticultural practices, so Hennemann has incorporated such considerations into the design. The structure's frame is apparently attuned to the vibrations of the earth, "helping to perpetuate the characteristics of all living things within the molecules of the wine". Even in bottle, the wines are stored at a precise horizontal, northeast orientation for streamlining with the land's energy forces. In an echo of both Lageder and Summerhill, Romanin says that its cellar "magnifies all the positive specificities of the wine it contains".

Like Summerhill, Romanin's dimensions reflect an Egyptian influence (in this case, their use of the royal cubit measurement, which was used to construct the pyramids at Giza) in the search for a singular environment for the wine.

A similar inspiration was used at Domaine Viret Clos du Paradis, where Philippe and Alain Viret's personal brand of the ancient made modern is known as Cosmoculture.

Cosmoculture, explain the Virets, is based on the knowledge of ancient civilizations such as the Maya and Inca. As with biodynamics, a balance is sought between earthly and cosmic forces – in this case, stone monoliths, or menhirs, in precise locations, transmit celestial energy into the ground, boosting the natural energies of the vines, and reducing the need for synthetic treatments. Homeopathic remedies are made from plants and rocks – materials that came from and return to the earth. They call it "alchemy rediscovered".

Their views are further demonstrated in the winery, which was built from three to six-ton stone blocks quarried in Vers and fitted into the winery structure in harmonious alignments. The nearby Pont du Gard aqueduct is made of similarly stern stuff. Oriented precisely according to the sun and a magnetic line that runs through the site, the winery has a simple but atmospheric interior reminiscent of a *basilica* or, as the Virets like to call it, a cathedral.

Philippe tells me that his aim is to make "living wines that continue to evolve in the bottle throughout their lives". His language is telling. As at Summerhill, Lageder, and Romanin, wine is seen as a living entity in a continuous state of evolution, from the vine to the glass. Respect for the soil, the

ANCIENT MADE MODERN

plant and the environment, as Philippe puts it, is directly expressed in the liquid. It is also reflected, though in very different ways, in all four wineries.

Just as Domaine Viret took inspiration from Inca culture, so another winery did a similar thing, but somewhat closer to home: Séptima, in Mendoza, Argentina. The comparison is revealing, if nothing else than to see how very different sizes and starting points can lead to similar building philosophies. Séptima is the seventh winery (hence the name) of the giant Spanish Codorníu group and, it can safely be said, is not into biodynamic production or Cosmoculture.

Yet to hear architect Eliana Bórmida speak of wanting "to convey the idea of an Andean temple and its associated ceremonies and rites" is not worlds away from the Virets' philosophy. Similar use of boulder-like local stone and an evocative cultural design enclosing a very ordered, functional space also link the two. Both wineries work on the twin levels of winemaking and cultural association. As Bórmida says, "we always try to link our buildings to a cultural past, and what better medium than wine to celebrate nature and the Earth?"

The symbolic function of Séptima also ties it in with another of Bórmida & Yanzón's wineries, Salentein (see p.59), also in Mendoza. At Salentein, Bórmida talks of celebrating Pachamama, the Andean earth goddess, by creating a barrel cellar in "the entrails of the earth". At Séptima, by contrast, the movement is upwards – as a symbolic Andean temple, it invites the visitor to climb the monumental staircases and contemplate the views of the distant Andes and surrounding vineyards from the top.

The materials used at Séptima were carefully chosen. For example, the oxidized ironwork around the smoked glass windows was selected to harmonize with the oxides in the 8,000 tons of locally quarried stone. And as the Andean uplands also contain rivers as well as rocks, the architects have placed rounded stones and natural grass at the front of the winery to break up the rigid lines.

Séptima ARGENTINA

Just as the interior is a highly functional, linear winemaking design, the exterior is strong in its symbolism, but also practical – the main façade is built for thermal isolation as well as earthquake resistance. It's not the most extrovert of wineries, but then it doesn't attempt to be.

The Incas were master stoneworkers. Impossibly large stone blocks fitted flush together with no mortar, just pure craftsmanship, into smooth surfaces over miles of walls in the most remote mountain territory. Another example of the finest stonework in the world can be seen at Macchu Picchu in Peru. Standing at Séptima is like hearing an echo of that Andean past in a modern winemaking environment. It was amusing to hear the architects' banter with Codorníu's Ricard Raventós when I visited. "You were asking us to build a shoe box," quipped Mario Yanzón. "And you managed to bring it to life," laughed Ricard.

Codorníu, being an international wine group, was keen to use local architects to create a regional identity for Séptima. Although many winery owners in an increasingly globalized wine business are indeed foreign, wine can champion the local cause like few other products can, both in the nature of its products and in the winery itself. Understandably keen to associate their products with a strong regional image, the more forward-thinking owners thus waste little time getting to know the vineyards, the terrain, and making sure their developments fit in. Ca' Marcanda, on Tuscany's Maremma seaboard, is one such example.

Angelo Gaja is hardly foreign. He's from long-standing northern Italian Piedmont stock, with a long family tradition of winemaking in Barbaresco. We often forget how fragmented Italy can be; the country was only unified in the 1860s and a strong sense of regionalism still often takes precedence over national unity. It's the Latin spirit – a sort of "my local cheese is better than your local cheese" kind of arrangement. It works the same with wine.

So when Gaja came to the calm undulations of Tuscany from the steep hills of Barbaresco, it was a big step. After planting vines in 1996, he looked to build

ANCIENT MADE MODERN

WINERIES WITH STYLE

Ca' Marcanda ITALY >>107, 110–11

ANCIENT MADE MODERN

a winery. He wanted a "landmark of new winery architecture" and yet integration in the landscape was also considered paramount. The facility was to cover a sizeable area and had by law to be at least seven metres (twenty-three feet) high in winemaking areas. Gaja called on architect Giovanni Bo.

"We were faced with the conflicting challenges of building a modern structure which would be compatible with such an ancient environment," muses Bo. The way he went about it was to initiate a detailed study of the environment ("the first and fundamental consideration") before designing the winery. He identified the local pattern of small hamlet-type farmhouse arrangements, interconnected yet isolated, and evidently warmed to their earthy appeal. He describes them as "simple in their geometry; the entire environment is distinguished by the delicate tonalities of nobly ageing plaster and stone." He also paid careful attention to the local vegetation and its colours.

All of these features are brought together in the winery. Built largely underground to minimize visual impact, Ca' Marcanda is like a mini-hamlet in itself. Buildings are clad in warm stone that was excavated from the site itself. Even the more modern touches are thought through: the tumbling iron and copper canopies over the entrance have been left untreated to oxidize and acquire a green-red hue similar to the surrounding vegetation. In a final touch, more than 250 ancient olive trees were replanted around the buildings to create, in Bo's words, "a time continuum". Ironically, this part of Italy has in recent times lost much of its typical landscape, as vines fast colonize the region, so it's good to see the local feel retained in a winery development.

Winery design does not always have to be restricted by local tradition, however. As well as foreign investors conforming to local rules, globalization also means a freedom for locals to adopt and adapt outside influences –

WINERIES WITH STYLE

Mission Hill CANADA

Domaine Viret Clos du Paradis (*see* p.105) is a case in point. It also holds true for Waterford in South Africa, which, while it's far from Tuscany, manages to engineer a serenely Tuscan impression.

The winery's distinct Mediterranean feel is evoked by features such as the neat citrus and lavender groves out front and the colonnaded central courtyard, with its centrepiece fountain. Warm tiles and multi-hued sandstone are combined with simple timber lintels, naturally cracked and contorted. When I arrived in the warming late-afternoon sunlight, the fountain was dribbling gently in the encroaching shadow. The soft tones of Coldplay wafted past miniature lavender pots;

ANCIENT MADE MODERN

Opus One USA

a dog dozed in the sun. It was a timeless sensation, removed from the banal bustle of everyday concerns.

The one thing that stops Waterford from being just another anonymous Tuscan transplant is the character imbued by winemaker Kevin Arnold. Waterford is largely the playing out of Arnold's winemaking vision, his "dream winery", in which architect Alex Walker has created a practical layout that exploits the concept of Mediterranean simplicity for its appeal. I ask Arnold to describe the winery's style. "It's Cape Mediterranean," he answers without hesitation. "People often forget that we have a Mediterranean climate in the Cape, and climate can be reflected in architecture just as it can in people's personalities."

Festive is not a word you would normally expect to hear a winemaker use of his winery, but Arnold is keen for people to experience the winemaking process at Waterford. The central courtyard has the feel of Italian family gatherings, while the four enclosing wings play host to the more functional aspects of wine. Suspended stainless-steel tanks peek out from one double doorway; small, high windows into the barrel cellar mark one wall. The arrangement is strikingly simple. "It's amazing that what is ultimately an industrial building can turn out like this," says a contented Arnold.

Much the same could be said of Mission Hill, overlooking Lake Okanagan in British Columbia, Canada, not too far away from Summerhill (see p.103). Like Waterford, Mission Hill is in keeping with a Mediterranean architectural influence, although its inspiration seems grander and more ancient. Summerhill took the architecture of ancient Egypt to winemaking extremes, and Mission Hill does the same with a modern take on Roman-style power and austerity.

The effect is dramatic. Owner Anthony von Mandl wanted a winery that was "an architectural statement unlike any other", and architect Tom Kundig went to town. Cellars were blasted out of the volcanic rock and a twelve-storey bell tower erected to form the centrepiece of the design. The two intersect in a piece of concrete geometric art. Outside, a courtyard is enclosed by the winery itself and a series of commanding, colonnaded structures that, along with the amphitheatre below, overlook the distant lake. Entrance to the courtyard is through a monumental concrete arch.

At first sight, Mission Hill does not appear to be architecture for those of a delicate disposition. But one of Kundig's main aims was in fact to create an experience that was complex and not immediately obvious. The concrete forms, for instance, initially seem bland but slowly reveal a delicate interplay of volumes and lines. The bell tower, both a historical reference and modern marker, is almost abstract in its simplicity and restrained features. Light is cast throughout the buildings in deliberate, almost minimalist fashion.

In what seems strange for such an imposing creation, Kundig also mentions how the architecture is designed to frame the natural surroundings like windows or thresholds. "We've tried to capture the tranquility of the space," he says. It is indeed a special location, and Kundig himself relates how he was captivated by the site on his first visit. Whether the resultant architecture does indeed play second fiddle to the landscape is debatable, but in Mandl's long-fought battle for recognition for Okanagan and Mission Hill, he now has a powerful tool in both the winery's location and its architecture.

South of British Columbia, Napa Valley in the USA is undoubtedly a global hotspot for showpiece wineries. While the concept was not invented here, it has been developed and instituted all along Route 29 in a manner reminiscent of the famous Las Vegas strip, where hotels tout for business with outrageous, magnificent pastiches of European architectural highlights. Napa's wine architecture, it must be admitted, falls a long way short of Vegas on the ostentation scale, but the Old World influence is still very much in evidence.

Approaching Opus One, it's difficult to tell whether this is a winery that courts attention or shuns it. On the one hand, you have the grassy berm, or

WINERIES WITH STYLE

Opus One USA ≫114, 118, 120–1

ANCIENT MADE MODERN 115

WINERIES WITH STYLE

Catena Zapata ARGENTINA >>121–3

ANCIENT MADE MODERN

Catena Zapata ARGENTINA

mound, that seems to shroud the winery, almost bury it under the land and vineyards. On the other, there are details like the striking cream limestone courtyard and colonnades, complete with fibreglass faux rocks that conceal speakers for piped music. It's an intriguing blend of extrovert Californian character and a more serene, classically European spirit.

This is explained by the fact that Opus One is a joint venture – pioneering at its time of founding in 1979 – between the French Rothschild family, of Château Mouton-Rothschild, and the Californian Robert Mondavi. Although the winery itself wasn't built until 1991, the fundamentals of the collaboration were by then well established and the challenge of moulding this hybrid vision into architectural form fell to Scott Johnson. It was not to copy either Mondavi or Mouton; it should be original, unpretentious, and yet incorporate Californian and French influences.

WINERIES WITH STYLE

Sterling USA >>123–5

ANCIENT MADE MODERN   119

Sterling USA

Patience was the first requirement for Johnson and his clients, as the design evolved over several years. It is interesting to note how Johnson now refers to the winery as "introverted, like a jewel box", alluding to how the structure is designed to entice the visitor in and only slowly reveal its character. The mix of styles is thought-provoking; some visitors liken it to Mayan or Egyptian architecture, others to a spaceship. As at Mission Hill, an attempt at timelessness was the idea.

The winery is essentially semi-circular in design, with a barrel cellar and glass-walled tasting room at the underground heart of the complex. Californian elements like redwood are juxtaposed with the European-style limestone courtyard; flowing circular motifs are fused with more formal, straight lines, such as in the striking central staircase. At all levels, Johnson has sought to marry a contemporary and classic feel, European and Californian aesthetic. Sometimes it falls into theatricality, as in the overly ornate salon, but, by and large, it's admirable architecture, in some places almost sculptural in its execution.

It's also popular with its inhabitants, which is always a good sign. My host Sandy, who had been working there for ten years, claimed never to have tired of any part of it. "It's soothing, sort of peaceful. It has its own character," she says, pausing thoughtfully before adding "and it makes working late hours and balancing budgets a whole lot less painful."

Opus One remains a landmark in the world of wine. When it was released in the early 1980s, its wine openly defied established Eurocentric views, and challenged the world's elite producers both in terms of price and quality. (The first vintage made, 1979, was still graceful and delicious in 2003.) It couldn't be written off simply as a New World upstart because of Mouton-Rothschild's participation; Mondavi was also winning praise for his pioneering work. The winery has become symbolic of that vision and has inspired other producers in more emerging areas around the world to follow Opus's lead.

Nicolás Catena, of Catena Zapata, freely admits to a "magic moment" of inspiration when he visited Mondavi's Napa operation in the early 1980s. The Argentine describes the experience as having radically changed his concept of winemaking – and, seeing as he took the tour, perhaps also impressed on him the potential benefits of self-promotion through a welcoming, iconic winery. The winemaking was what occupied Catena at first on his return to Mendoza, Argentina; the winery would have to wait until 2001 for its debut. But when it came, it did so in typically provocative fashion.

The winery was built as a Mayan pyramid. The question Catena had faced was how to build a winery that would encapsulate both his winemaking aspirations and a regional identity. His aim, like that of Opus One and many others before him, was to put his relatively unknown region on the international wine map. He wanted something new, different, and zany, yet which people could associate with Argentina, or at least Latin America.

The Maya, according to architecture critic Jonathan Glancey, are more closely associated with Central America, where their monumental pyramids are the earliest examples of such structures on the American continent. Like the Aztecs, it appears these structures were used for religious ceremonies, which included regular human sacrifice. The Maya were among the most advanced and literate of meso-American cultures, and, although it appears they never developed the wheel, were experts in astronomy, calculation of time, mathematics, geometry, and farming.

It was with this heritage that Nicolás Catena chose to associate himself and his winery. Even the surrounding vineyard was named Uxmal, after the Mayan settlement in Mexico. Standing on the pyramid top, surveying the vineyards and mountains beyond, winemaker Pepe Galante jokes "if Nicolás doesn't like the wines, I'll be the one sacrificed on this pyramid". Monumental bronze studded doors lead into the building and light filters down from the central roof skylight, scattered decoratively by a series of diagonal metal staircases.

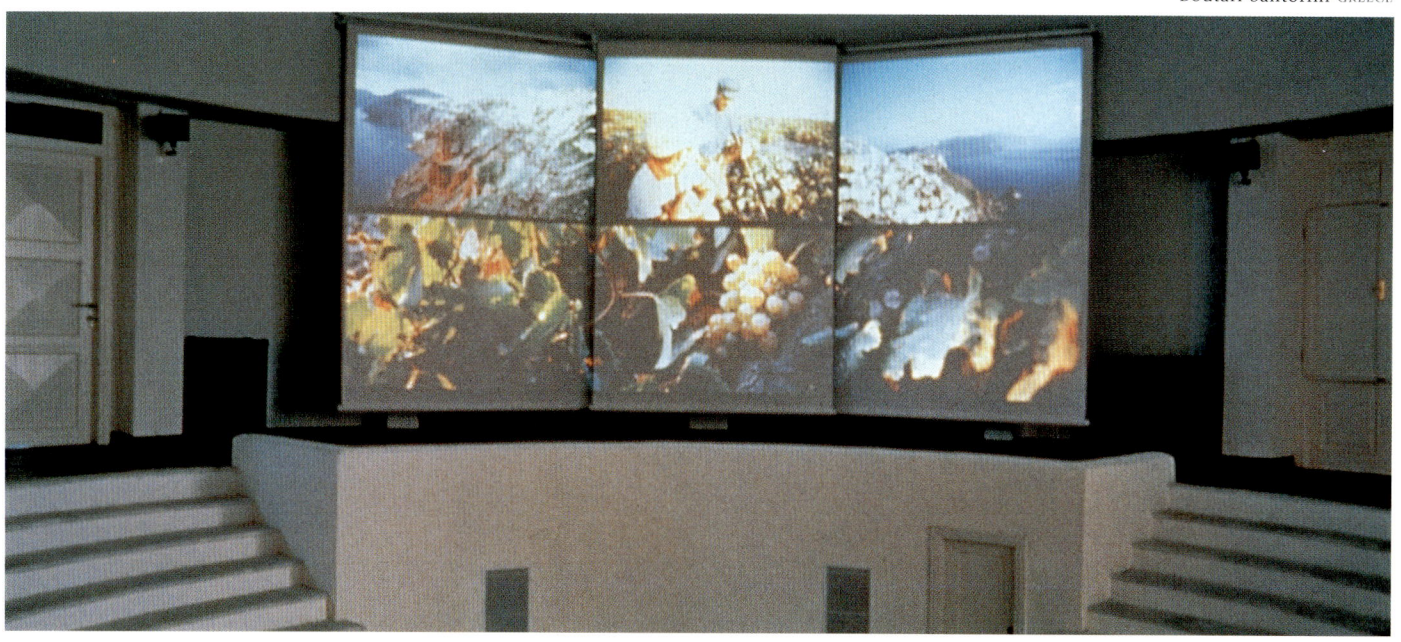

But the influences at Catena Zapata go beyond the Maya. The semi-circular barrel cellar and accompanying glass-panelled tasting room is a direct reference to Opus One. So, too, the central, circular void that gives the progression down to the cellar a ceremonial air. Through these devices, it seems Catena is stating his ambition for the wines to rank among the best in the world. The architecture not only places Catena Zapata in Latin America, but it also plays to a wider, more international audience.

Well before even Catena and Mondavi, however, a winery named Sterling had been built on top of a ninety-metre (300-foot) knoll at the northern end of Napa Valley. It broke new ground in many ways, not least of which was a bold attempt to make an architectural statement that would attract and intrigue passers-by at a time in the early 1970s when there was little concept of visiting wineries. The model for this gleaming white calling-card was Greek, a Mykonoan monastery.

It was, perhaps, ironic that such a high-profile invitation to visit was inspired by a monastery – the Greek term for "living alone". But Englishman Peter Newton, who first established Sterling, was committed to democratizing wine; he opened the winery in 1972, and the visitor centre in 1973. In one of the many quirky touches at the winery, he brought eight bells from the war-torn church of St Dunstan's, near the Tower of London, to hang in the bell towers at the winery. The religious associations of the place were further enhanced when the bells were blessed on Ascension Day in 1973.

The Greek theme is said to have been inspired by Napa's Mediterranean climate. Sterling certainly seems at home on its wooded hilltop location, its bright white form framed by the deep blue sky, russet earth, and dark green trees, including two obelisk-like cypresses standing to attention at the southern wall. It is made up of a collection of buildings that have commanding views over the valley, both to the south and north.

Sterling's views are reached not by conventional stairs, though. Instead, there is a cable car – or, as my genial guide Don termed it, a tram. The earnest, bustling Don later informed me in conspiratorial tones that the tram was to comply with stringent disability laws guaranteeing every visitor the same experience. The tram is indeed an experience in its own right, swaying gently

Shadowfax AUSTRALIA >>126

Shadowfax AUSTRALIA

over trees and landscaped ponds – for some visitors, mainly the smaller kind, it's a reason to visit in itself.

"I graduated from Calistoga High in 1963 and back then this was a small, sleepy area," says Don, peering timidly out across the valley towards Calistoga from the terrace. "Then Sterling came along and surprised everyone with this winery. It made everybody sit up and take notice." I ask him what he made of the architecture when it first went up. "Oh," he grins sheepishly, "that depends on the person. It depends on the culture."

Culture is exactly what Boutari's Santorini winery is all about. Santorini is a small, rugged, and wind-swept island just a few miles away from Mykonos in the Cyclades. The local architecture isn't too different either – villages huddle together on precipitous cliffs, a jumble of clean white lines between the deep blue sea and sky. Where Sterling is a foreign reflection of this Greek style, Boutari Santorini is inspired by a home-grown type of Greek architecture.

"The design was meticulously worked out to fit the traditional Cycladic architecture with modern materials," says winemaker Yannis Voyatzis. The winery was sunk into the volcanic rock to minimize visual impact, and a *tholos*, or domed conference centre, with an interior like a mini-amphitheatre, was incorporated to break up the stern lines. It is an arrangement reminiscent of the way vines are cultivated on the island, which is in a unique basket shape to protect against the wind and retain every drop of precious moisture. Like the vines, the small collection of winery buildings sits low in the blustery landscape, overlooking the Aegean Sea and the island's crater rim.

The crater points to Santorini's past as part of a huge volcano that is thought to have undergone a cataclysmic eruption in 1500BC. Now, however, the bleak volcanic soils are hospitable to only two things: vines and tourists. But with easy money coming from tourism, many wine growers are turning their backs on centuries of tradition, and land is being swallowed up by developers. I spoke to one old hand who painted a picture as bleak as the island. "No one cares,"

ANCIENT MADE MODERN

Shadowfax AUSTRALIA

he said. "Already it's the old people left to do this back-breaking work and soon all the vineyard land will be sold. I don't know if we can stop this."

So it's good to see the likes of Boutari fighting to preserve this ancient winemaking tradition. Marina Boutari defines one of the new winery's purposes as "preserving the unique legacy and tradition of this astonishing land". Even the local vine, Assyrtiko, is an age-old inheritance. Greece has, in recent years, been a land of winemaking renaissance, led by the likes of Boutari, which controls wineries all over the country. Santorini deserves to be at the heart of that revival.

If Santorini boasts an architecture that rises from its volcanic earth, then Australia has a similar proposition in the Shadowfax winery in Victoria. The building has been designed to look like a steel and glass tunnel hemmed in by mounds of earth, its rusted sheet metal exterior coloured like the soil. It recalls a no-nonsense Australian winemaking heritage (one Aussie winemaker once laughingly described his country's wineries to me as "tin sheds and iron shacks") yet drawn together in what is a remarkably innovative piece of architecture.

Architects Roger Wood and Randal Marsh talk of taking a sculptural approach to the building to distance it from associations with "factories or galleries". The angle of the external lateral walls is designed to mimic the shape of bulldozed or ploughed earth when it comes to rest; the oxidized finish a further integrating factor. The sloping wedges are interspersed with glass windows for views both in and out. Mesh panels break up the hard lines and create dappled shade. The idea is that the winery appears to be fashioned from the earth itself, not simply positioned on site.

Shadowfax is the name of the chief of horses in J.R.R. Tolkien's *Lord of the Rings*, a steed that spurns all but the finest riders, shining by day and passing unseen at night. The contrast between exhibitionism and discretion is reflected in the progression from the winery's subdued exterior into a vibrant, vivid interior, full of light and modernity. Brightly coloured geometric screens frame the space and an orange spiral staircase leads down into the wide vaulted cellar. Portholes in the floor allow light to filter through and link the winemaking process to the drinking process at the bar.

The brief at Shadowfax was for the architects to create a "contemporary, striking, and fully functional winery" that would enable workers and visitors to feel "comfortable and inspired". The architects have responded with a winery that makes reference to the land and an Australian style of vernacular architecture, but seems to take on more lofty aspirations beyond its station, a sort of admirable overambition.

Chile's Viña Gracia combines the same rural simplicity with a sense of ambition, artistry, and fun. A modular facility in the same vein as Shadowfax, Gracia could just be another industrial, rural shed or barn were it not for architect Germán del Sol's inspired details.

For what is essentially a very simple warehouse structure, del Sol started by designing an exterior of plunging timber interspersed with clear strips. The effect is not just to break up the regularity of the building, but, more importantly, to transform the environment with light. Inside, the hard lines of inert winemaking equipment are brought to life by constantly moving daylight. At night, light falls in stripes outside. The connection between the building and its environment is conducted through a delicate light interchange.

Although Gracia is scrupulously functional inside, the architect has inserted two structures that lift the interior above the purely practical. The lime green facility for tasting, offices, and labs is a flamboyant piece of asymmetric timber design, with a curved façade, and the feel of a nautical vessel inside. The stairs run in diagonal fashion across the front in a design similar to that of the barrel cellar walls, where small oblique openings have been cut into the wood to break up an otherwise regular appearance.

WINERIES WITH STYLE

Gracia CHILE >>126-7

"It's like a kid with a bike – deconstructing reality in order to understand it, play with it, and then put it back together," says del Sol of his creative process. A fierce advocate of overcoming "deep-rooted prejudices about what things 'should be,'" the architect has indeed defied tradition at Gracia, while at the same time giving new life to an ancient format: the warehouse. He talks of how his use of light at Gracia imbues the winemaking process with "grace and poetry".

The word *gracia* in Spanish has a dual meaning: grace and humour. Gracia's ethos seems to be based on defying wine convention, from its asymmetric slash labels, to its slogan inviting the consumer to "experience the south side of life". Even the winery's architecture gets in on the act. This lively, cavalier attitude is summed up in the following cheeky rationale, on the winery's website: "Tradition does not spring from the domaines of a medieval château, but from the repeated vocation of human beings to sit around a table, to drink, and to share. The tradition for Gracia may go back 6,000 years. Was Noah the precursor?"

ANCIENT MADE MODERN 127

IN BRIEF

ALOIS LAGEDER LOWENGANG
Alto Adige, Italy
BUILT 1995 by Abram & Schnabl
WINE TIP Contest Hirschprunn
VISITS By appointment
www.lageder.com

Lageder has so much to offer that it's almost impossible to summarize. But I'll have a go. Art, architecture, wine, mountains, beehives, Bach. All good. How does that sound?

SUMMERHILL
Okanagan, British Columbia, Canada
BUILT 1997 by Stephen Cipes
WINE TIP Summerhill Meritage
VISITS Open doors
www.summerhill.bc.ca

Does wine age better in a pyramid? Summerhill thinks so – and I'm open to persuasion after tasting their delicious wines. Also, look out for the new Enchanted Vines series; they come complete with fancy artwork and a shaman's blessing.

ROMANIN
Les Baux-de-Provence, France
BUILT 1992 by Serge Hennemann
WINE TIP Romanin 2000
VISITS Open doors
www.romanin.com

Provençal wine struggles to lose the image of shoddy holiday rosé, mainly because most of it still is. There are, however, producers doing more serious and interesting things, such as the biodynamic Romanin.

DOMAINE VIRET CLOS DU PARADIS
Rhône, France
BUILT 1999 by Cabinet Arc
WINE TIP Maréotis
VISITS By appointment
www.domaine-viret.com

Where Romanin practises biodynamics, Viret is into Cosmoculture. Both systems aim to treat vines and fruit with maximum respect, both in the vineyard and winery – and to produce wines with a touch of magic.

SEPTIMA
Mendoza, Argentina
BUILT 2001 by Bórmida & Yanzón
WINE TIP Séptima Syrah
VISITS By appointment
www.bodegaseptima.com.ar

Séptima is the seventh winery – hence the name – of Spanish wine group Codorníu, better known for its Cava. Still a young operation, Séptima's architecture has already given it impeccable Argentine credentials.

CA' MARCANDA
Tuscany, Italy
BUILT 2002 by Giovanni Bo
WINE TIP Promis
VISITS By appointment

A Tuscan venture by Barbaresco legend Angelo Gaja, Ca' Marcanda means "long negotiation" in Piedmont dialect. The new winery blends discreetly into its venerable surroundings. Expectations are high as Gaja attempts to match the Super Tuscan wines from this region.

WATERFORD
Helderberg, Stellenbosch, South Africa
BUILT 2000 by Alex Walker
WINE TIP Kevin Arnold Shiraz
VISITS Open doors
www.waterfordwines.com

Winemaker Kevin Arnold's wines are usually something special, and the winery he has helped create at Waterford is no different. It has a distinctly Mediterranean feel, relaxing and serene, with some excellent wines to hand.

Catena Zapata ARGENTINA

Waterford SOUTH AFRICA

Boutari Santorini GREECE

MISSION HILL
Okanagan, British Columbia, Canada
BUILT 2002 by Olson Sundberg Kundig Allen
WINE TIP Pinot Blanc
VISITS Open doors
www.missionhillwinery.com

A stunning location and imposing architecture is part of owner Anthony von Mandl's grand plan for worldwide recognition for his local Okanagan region. The other big part of the plan, the wines, are coming along fine.

OPUS ONE
Napa Valley, USA
BUILT 1991 by Johnson Fain Partners
WINE TIP Opus One 1995
VISITS By appointment
www.opusonewinery.com

Opus is a musical term, but here it refers to the pioneering work of the Rothschilds and Robert Mondavi, who, in forging a ground-breaking venture in 1979, broadened the horizons of the New World. Wines are excellent, if pricey.

CATENA ZAPATA
Mendoza, Argentina
BUILT 2001 by Pablo Sánchez Elias
WINE TIP Argento Bonarda Reserva
VISITS By appointment
www.catenawines.com

Catena owes a debt to both Mondavi and the Mayan civilization. Mondavi inspired Catena's winemaking policy; a Mayan pyramid was the model for the winery. The result is some of Argentina's best wine.

STERLING
Napa Valley, USA
BUILT 1972 by Martin Waterfield
WINE TIP Winery Lake Chardonnay
VISITS Open doors
www.sterlingvineyards.com

Since being founded by Englishman Peter Newton in the 1960s, Sterling has passed through the hands of such large drinks groups as Coca-Cola, Seagram, and now Diageo. Still producing wines of character and elegance.

BOUTARI SANTORINI
Santorini, Greece
BUILT 1989 by Yiannis Yianniotis
WINE TIP Kallisti barrel fermented Assyrtiko
VISITS Open doors
www.boutari.gr

Boutari has wineries all over Greece, but its Santorini operation is a jewel in the portfolio. Nonetheless, Santorini's historic Assyrtiko vineyards are under threat from encroaching tourist developments. Help by drinking.

SHADOWFAX
Geelong, Victoria, Australia
BUILT 2000 by Wood Marsh
WINE TIP Geelong Pinot Noir
VISITS Open doors
www.shadowfax.com.au

The name is evocative and so is the winery, proof that Australia can do funky architecture that makes reference to its own history and natural elements. All wines come highly recommended.

GRACIA
Cachapoal, Chile
BUILT 1997 by Germán del Sol
WINE TIP Porqueno Cabernet Sauvignon
VISITS By appointment
www.gracia.cl

Although Gracia employs a French winemaker, its style is very much hip New World. Owned by the well-endowed Córpora group, the winery has access to fruit from all over Chile.

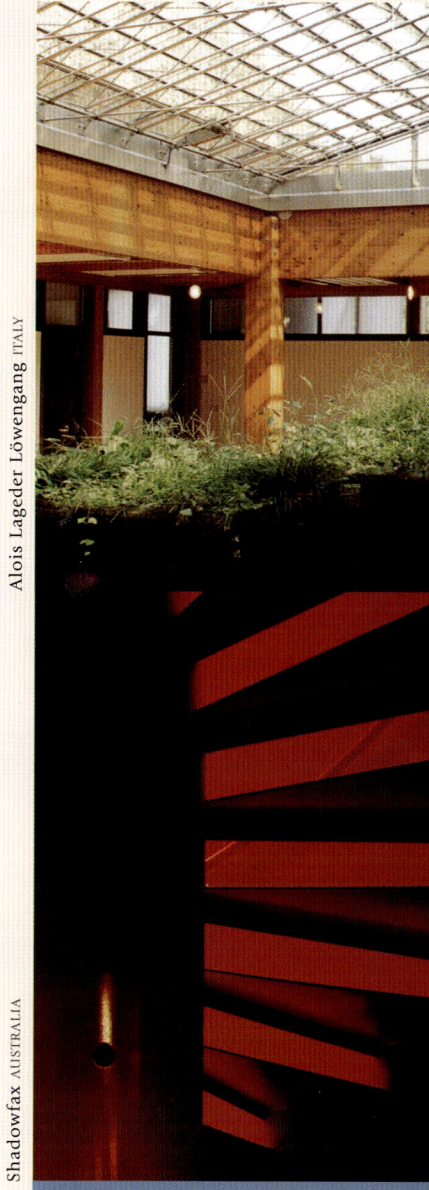

Alois Lageder Löwengang ITALY

Shadowfax AUSTRALIA

Summerhill CANADA

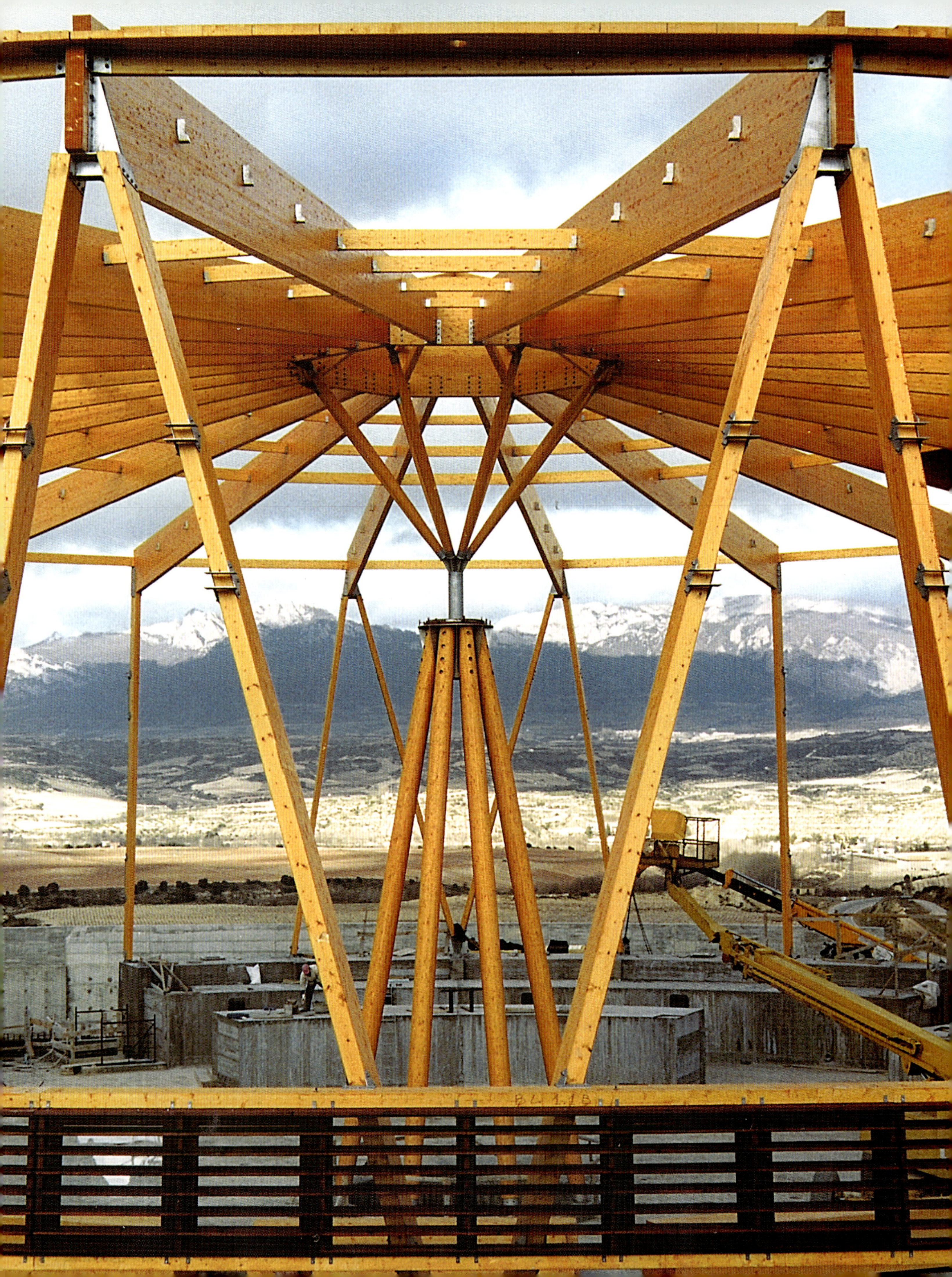

IMMACULATE CONCEPTIONS

WINERIES THAT LAY WINEMAKING BARE

Ban-hus was an expression in Old English. It meant body – the bone house. It's a little piece of prose turned poetry; the naked human frame made architecture. Working parts, industry, mechanics – so essential, so often hidden – can also be made beautiful, and central features in the wine house.

Viña Real SPAIN

When, in 1887, Gustave Eiffel began building the Eiffel Tower in Paris, it was denounced by many as a monstrosity. An open letter was penned by a group of enraged intellectuals comparing it to the tower of Babel and slating the tower as ridiculous, profane, and – most galling of all for Eiffel – useless.

Eiffel's response was clinical, his words straight from the textbook of great architecture. "I believe the tower will have its own beauty," he replied in clipped tones. "Just because we're engineers, do people think beauty does not concern us; that while we build for solidity and durability we do not strive for elegance?"

The great engineer also pointed to the tower's potential application in the fields of physics, astronomy, meteorology, and radio broadcasting. Deep down, though, Eiffel was just proud at having created a building that celebrated the great advancements of his age, one that would ultimately come to symbolize Paris and France itself. He wrote with scarcely concealed delight at how he had heard the tower had captured the imagination of those as far away as China and India. This alone was justification enough for him.

Although Eiffel did dabble in the architecture of wine (see González-Byass, p.48–51), it was his wider message that would ultimately come to illuminate the wine world. Coupling a solid sense of purpose with a capacity to delight is never easy, but wineries that manage it can enjoy the best of both worlds: efficient production and instant recognition.

"You see, it's all about combining practicality with great design," says Juan Carlos García Sedano, stepping neatly over a pile of dusty cabling and into the vinification hall. His thick Castilian monologue continues but, as soon as we enter this soaring place, he has lost me. It's huge. Strikingly circular, warm from the wooden roof and walls but clinical with the concrete and stainless steel tanks. At the centre, what looks like an enormous tepee skeleton, as if the sky has sent down roots, and at the apex the horizontal arm of a crane clutches tightly. Light filters gently onto the scene through a central skylight and squinting windows. Juan's words echo in my ear: practicality with great design.

We're at the brand new Viña Real winery in Rioja. Originally simply a vineyard and brand, Viña Real's owners CVNE decided the time was ripe for an iconic new winery to coincide with their 125th anniversary in 2004. After French architect Philippe Mazières was given a prominent hillside location, he designed the new facility in a flowing, three-part design that culminates in what appears to be a giant wooden fermenting vat. At least, that's the idea. Inside the *tina* (Spanish for vat – also a handy nickname for the building) is the colossal vinification hall Juan and I are now standing in.

He patiently explains. The crane is a CVNE invention. It hoists little metal pods (jokingly called OVIs, Identified Flying Objects) that can be filled with grapes or juice and emptied into any of the tanks, thanks to the circular layout. It saves time, energy, and allows for greater control over the winemaking. The windows and skylight control the entry of light, not just into the hall, but also into the barrel cellar below via a round glass panel in the floor. This barrel cellar is also arranged in circular fashion, with slanted concrete columns, reminiscent of Bofill's version for Lafite-Rothschild (see p.51). The barrels can be moved quickly and efficiently into two adjacent tunnels bored into the hillside. Simple.

132 WINERIES WITH STYLE

Viña Real SPAIN

And yet, in its simple practicality, Viña Real is exhilarating. What is to all intents and purposes a fairly humdrum, though original, winemaking system has been invested with a keen sense of drama by the architect. Other elements in the facility, such as the curvaceous middle building and cavernous tunnels, merely serve as warm-up acts to the practical heart of the winery.

The traditional heartlands of Rioja are ablaze with architectural invention. It's not, of course, just about making wineries more practical. It's about making a statement, just as Eiffel did, to draw attention to what the practicality serves. Juan Carlos talks of "creating an axis of tourism for wine and architecture", alluding to stunning nearby wineries such as Marqués de Riscal (see p.167) and Ysios (see p.166), as well as Frank Gehry's famous Bilbao Guggenheim Museum. If the latter has given Bilbao a new lease of life, why not do the same for wine, runs the logic, and more specifically Riojan wine?

Raising the mechanics of winemaking into a more artistic plane is something Jacques Lardière is familiar with. As Louis Jadot's chief winemaker, the gifted Lardière oversees a dizzying array of Burgundian wines (more than 150 labels are produced by Jadot each vintage) and his ingenious repartee can have a similarly intoxicating effect.

IMMACULATE CONCEPTIONS 133

WINERIES WITH STYLE

Louis Jadot La Sablière FRANCE >>136, 138

IMMACULATE CONCEPTIONS

Craggy Range NEW ZEALAND ≫138

When I quizzed Lardière about Jadot's stunning La Sablière winery, he genially talked me through concepts such as "dynamizing the biomass" and "aromatic extensions". The winery is arranged in a circular layout, concentric circles of tanks below a series of rotating arms and a soaring timber roof. At the centre stands a chestnut-wood platform, the focus of radiating zig-zag lines built into the floor, an acoustic epicentre. This is surely Lardière's soapbox.

"Life is organized from left to right, in lines. But if you follow the pattern around, you create a spiral, and that can dynamize molecules. In creating the circular tank and roof design, we encourage an aromatic aspiration in the wine that promotes purity, subtlety, and delicacy. It imbues the mechanics of ageing in the wine, enabling it to mature and take on new character. Because what is a great vineyard but a place that will dynamize its wine's molecules and enable it to transform with age?" Hesitantly, I ask him whether he finds the winery practical. "Yup, we think it works pretty well."

WINERIES WITH STYLE

Craggy Range NEW ZEALAND

IMMACULATE CONCEPTIONS 137

Terre da Vino ITALY

The circular winemaking design is similar in concept to that at Viña Real, even if the philosophies differ in their expression. So, why have so many wineries taken to working in the round in recent times? It seems to be a curious balance between efficiency and a drive for harmonious design. While the use of space can certainly be more wasteful in circular cellars, and the work more dizzying for cellar workers, it does encourage a certain type of efficiency. Eric de Rothschild of Lafite-Rothschild (*see* p.51) is convinced that it saves an enormous amount of man-hours in terms of rolling barrels. "Sure, it's more complicated working in a circle," Juan Carlos at Viña Real told me, "and more expensive to make the right size tanks, but it will ultimately be more efficient." Its natural, less industrial edge also has many fans, not the least being Lardière.

The key aspect at Jadot, though, is the way Burgundy's mazy patchwork of vineyards is reflected in the profusion of tanks. In a region like Burgundy, where the character of wines can differ enormously from vines just yards apart, a great deal of fragmentation is necessary in any serious winemaking process. That means a hive of activity at harvest time, and lots of individual tanks to attend to. Given Jadot's size, and with holdings all over Burgundy, the system needs to be exactly right.

Lardière and Jadot succeed admirably in their task of making hundreds of different wines, each with a different character that reflects its vineyard. As I was told when I visited, "this winery helps us put our winemaking philosophy into physical form." Lardière insists on minimizing human intervention in order to let the grapes express themselves – this fundamentally practical challenge is where La Sablière comes into its own.

Attention to single-vineyard sites in the winemaking process is also a hallmark of the Craggy Range winery in New Zealand. In fact, the winery only makes wines produced from single vineyards, which are scattered over various key regions including Hawke's Bay, Martinborough, and Marlborough. It's not often that the New World goes in so wholeheartedly for what the French term the expression of terroir, but in their Giants Winery complex, Craggy Range has even named their sugar pot of a restaurant after it.

Winemaking director and Master of Wine Steve Smith defines terroir as the complex interplay of geology, soil, climate, and culture. Significantly, he also adds that "terroir can only be shown when the human hand plays a gentle but highly skilled and decisive role in the vineyards and winery." It's a credo that has much in common with Lardière at Jadot, and at the Giants Winery the winemaking ethos is similarly based around gentle handling and parcel selection. For some wines, grapes are picked from the same vineyard at different times, vinified and aged apart before later being blended. This takes skill, experience, and, not least, a lot of space.

Nonetheless, for the Giants Winery complex, neither Smith nor architect John Blair wanted an imposing structure that would jar with the landscape. The result is a series of buildings that have been carefully composed as both individually functioning units and a coherent whole. Shapes, colours, and materials have been designed to complement each other, yet each facility performs a definite task: red wine fermentation, offices, restaurant, visitor centre. The architecture has a fresh, functional feel to it – Smith was keen to convey a practical yet modern image, a gesture to tradition but not subservience to it.

Such freedom and freshness in formal design is not often found in the smallholding heartlands of European wine-growing areas. This is what makes the likes of Jadot and Viña Real special – a commitment to making the nuts and bolts of the winemaking process the bold centre of attention in what otherwise might have been an introverted wine estate. It speaks of a certain transparency.

Another winery doing its bit for transparent winemaking is Terre da Vino, amid hillsides steeped in tradition in Italy's northwestern corner of Barolo in Piedmont. The architecture conveys it at a glance in the abundance of glass, light, and an open plan linked by a suspended walkway. This device – quaintly termed a "flying passageway" – enables the visitor to get a bird's eye view of the winemaking process without disturbing proceedings. It also passes outside, giving fine vistas over the surrounding hills and vineyards. Bold use of colour and a delicate interplay of curved and triangular wooden roofing sets the complex of buildings firmly in its local landscape.

What makes Terre da Vino's achievement all the more astounding is that it is one of Italy's largest cooperative cellar associations. Some 2,500 growers farm 3,900 hectares of vines and all the wine produced (about 4.2 million bottles of it) conforms to strict Piedmontese appellation of origin requirements. Its size, though, has been transformed into an asset – the architectural effect in some places is derived from sheer scale, as in the barrel hall where the huge arched wooden roof echoes the shape and quantity of barrels below.

The impression is of lightness, modernity, and innovation. Which, for a substantial cooperative, is probably just the job. The company optimistically forecasts that the new winery will "contribute without doubt to make us well known" for what marketing manager Cristina Torrengo defines as "the marriage between technology and tradition". It's a simple, striking formula made all the more prominent, owing to its traditional location.

When I visited Burgundy, another great traditional, fragmented winemaking region, I took the opportunity to meet up with a couple of former architects, now turned very successful winemakers. I asked them how they viewed the relationship between architecture and wine. The charming Jean-Charles Le Bault de la Morinière told me "'God is in the detail', as Mies van der Rohe said. Architecture prepares you for precision and detail, which helps in winemaking. Sure, you must also have an ability for abstraction, but it's the organizational aspect I prize most." Fabio Gazeau-Montrasi, meanwhile, explained: "there's a tendency to be too monumental in winery architecture. I prefer the sober, functional feel – buildings that inspire great passion are rarely very functional."

Naturally, both Jean-Charles' and Fabio's wineries (Bonneau du Martray and Château des Rontets, respectively) are the epitome of sober functionalism – as, in fact, were all former architects' facilities I called in at (there are a surprising number in the wine industry). But you get the feeling that if they were to design a winery from scratch, and in a place like New Zealand, it could end up being something like Ransom.

Ransom is a perfect example of a strong, simple and pragmatic winery, just like the local New Zealand character. And that, says architect Graeme Scott, was just the idea. "The form of the building avoids any references to traditional European masonry wineries, preferring instead to create an appropriate New Zealand architecture of openness and light, well sited in the natural landscape." Building materials are uncomplicated – steel, wood, concrete. A spacious gallery runs right through the heart of the winery, bringing the outside in and allowing people to experience everything, from winemaking to the bar and restaurant terrace.

"The design is pure contemporary New Zealand," enthuses owner Robin Ransom, "without reference to other times and places, which places us pretty much in the here and now." He does not, however, distance himself from tradition in winemaking terms, saying instead that in the architecture of Ransom they have created a type of equilibrium between tradition and modernity that is also captured in the wines. "Our task is to reflect what is best in Old World winemaking and wine styles, by which I mean treating wine as a partner with

WINERIES WITH STYLE

food rather than as a stand-alone 'look at me' product, and making elegant wines which will age with grace and style."

Ransom is not a "look at me" type of winery, which is precisely its appeal. Wine has been stripped down to its essentials in a forthright and logical winery that sits easily in its rural location. This sort of approachable charm is easy to overlook – though, paradoxically, it can be turned to good effect. Ransom, Robin tells me, has been featuring prominently in a local TV drama. "Visitors recognize it with a mixture of surprise and delight when they arrive," he says, excitedly. In a recent move, the winery also now stars in pen and ink on the wine labels.

In Bordeaux, a sense of modernity and freedom is slightly harder to contrive. The weight of tradition can be oppressive. When the Leda group under Jean-Jacques Lesgourgues came to build Château Haut Selve in the Graves appellation, however, the aim was to resist the urge of history. Leda's Bernard Matabos defines Haut Selve's particular style as "a permanent call to creativity", adding: "everything is possible. There's no dogma, no barriers to experimentation and a questioning mind."

If described in terse and unflattering terms, the winery could come across as hideous: pink prefab concrete meets a low-slung, functional, boxy design. But the credit due to architect Sylvain Dubuisson is that he has made just such a structure into an engaging piece of architecture.

As Jean-Charles said, it's all about the detail. Dubuisson has the winemaking process at the heart of the design, running the length of this long building in familiar linear fashion. It's this that forms the core of the structure; everything else grows from here. Though the vinification hall is meticulously symmetrical, the adjacent barrel cellar has a livelier touch, with yawning concrete arches and a timber-clad interior. Light and shadow are used to atmospheric effect, which is partly owing to a feature best appreciated from the outside.

The prefabricated concrete elements include a series of windows that varies from long vertical slits to chunky squares. As well as lighting the interior, these break up the façades in understated fashion. It's a complex but subtle geometry, also captured in the gentle slopes of the walls and roof. Kept low to the ground to avoid jarring with the vines and trees around, the winery sports a surprising, raised grille roof over its central atrium or courtyard. The idea, in the architect's words, is to give what is otherwise a thoroughly entrenched building a sense of lightness.

Enlightening touches also come courtesy of sculptors Vincent Barré and Juan Bordes, the latter having designed mythological figures Castor and Pollux to frame the entrance to the atrium. Even the winery has a certain sculptural quality to it. So is this the new style of architecture for Bordeaux? Matabos is pragmatic. "Our motto is '*Non nova sed Nove*' – not new things, but things done in a new way. The respect for terroir in our wines is fundamental – the modernity and technology is simply there to aid that natural expression."

Clean lines, natural light, plenty of space, and an undisturbed working environment is what makes for a happy winemaker, according to Ian Naudé of Dornier in South Africa. "Even my toolbox is on wheels," he jokes, breaking into one of his characteristic, hearty chuckles that causes his wine to slosh. Looking around, it's easy to see what he means. Suspended stainless steel tanks and high windows make for a spacious, light work-place. The windows also allow visitors to see in without interrupting the winemaking.

"I saw a book on New York lofts and thought – this is what I want," says Naudé. "It's clean and easy, there's nothing to work around. It's simple – I just want to make wine, and it doesn't come much simpler than this." And yet Dornier, like Haut Selve, is more than just a winemaker's functional fantasy.

WINERIES WITH STYLE

Owner and artist Christoph Dornier worked with architect Johan Malherbe to dress Naudé's vision in more inventive garb.

They came up with an undulating rooftop and frontispiece pond that, when seen together, form a reflective picture. Naudé is quick to point out that the pond has a practical application in cooling the barrel cellar below, but it fulfils an aesthetic purpose, too, framing the winery and weathered mountains behind. Opposite the winery stands a series of traditional Cape Dutch buildings with whitewashed walls and thatched roofs. Dornier was express in his desire for the winery not to ape such traditional architecture, but Malherbe still had to blend the building into its context.

The answer was a straightforward structure made from basic materials that works well in its situation – Malherbe cites the American architectural master Frank Lloyd Wright's advocacy of simple materials in his design. The scene is best surveyed from the winery's central terrace, where Cape Dutch gables peek over a trough in the roof's curvature. The view directly into the stainless steel of the winemaking process is contrasted with a panorama over the valley and mountains beyond.

The twentieth century saw much in the way of rational design in architecture. Some such buildings stood the test of time; others, like many high-rise apartment blocks, fell from grace and suffered architecture's most ignoble end: demolition. The sort of rational, highly functional design of the era had a spiritual home in the Bauhaus, in Germany. The Bauhaus was not just an architectural statement in its own right, it was also a school where successful architects studied and taught, including the king of detail, Mies van der Rohe.

Although the Bauhaus was only a brief phenomenon, its influence was huge. So, to hear my host Martin Schwegler describe Staatsweingut Weinsberg's new cellars as "more Bauhaus than Baroque", as he disappears into a concrete monochrome office, seems entirely appropriate. Here is a thoroughly rational winery, built from strong, simple materials, alternately solid and transparent, with colour-coded levels and a winemaking process exemplary in its efficiency. Not only that – Weinsberg, like the Bauhaus, is also a school. It is state funded and specializes in wine and viticulture.

The Baroque reference was because the Weinsberg wine school is the oldest such establishment in Germany, dating back to 1868, and historical structures still exist on the site. But Weinsberg's proudest recent acquisition is its new winery. Not only does it serve the purposes of professional winemaking in the usual manner, but in this case it also takes on added role – that of classroom.

Weinsberg is a kind of dream kindergarten, where the only subject taught is wine. Everything is geared toward learning – from the profusion of small-scale equipment, to room names in the corridors, and winemaking diagrams on the walls. All that's missing, you sense, is a sandpit. And Weinsberg doesn't disappoint. The barrel cellar introduces a few lighter touches to the otherwise disciplined atmosphere of the winery, one of which is an art display featuring a pool of sand combed by a long pendulum. Martin explains that it symbolizes time passing as the wine slowly evolves, and the sand evokes the soil in the vineyard. A nearby water and wood feature recalls the rain and the vines.

A similar lightness of touch is evident in the winery's shop, also modernist in style, with its flat roof and glass walls that create a light, airy feel within which wine is displayed on artistic stands. "This was all a long time coming," says Martin, gesturing to the winery and shop. "First in the planning, then after German reunification the state was broke; in the end it was only through the influence of former pupils we managed to get the funding pushed through." He pauses. "But it's a fine thing to have a new house, no?"

In Jancis Robinson and Hugh Johnson's *The World Atlas of Wine*, Baden and Württemberg, where Weinsberg is located, is lauded in the following terms: "Nowhere in Germany has the rationalization and modernization of the wine industry gone further and faster." At Weinsberg, Schwegler is keen to point out that such modernization is not just confined to the winemaking and viticulture, but also includes the architecture. "It's important that people see this calm, professional modern environment," he says, "because at the end of the day this is a state-owned establishment – and these people are our taxpayers."

South Africa's rationalization process only started in earnest in the latter half of the 1990s, following the end of apartheid. The Cape was suddenly thrown open to international influences – though as one burly wine producer reminded me in no uncertain terms: "we South Africans are bloody good at playing catch-up". As with Weinsberg, that modernization process has found expression in the winery architecture.

Avant-garde architect Johan Wessels has built two wineries for Graham Beck, the most recent of which is the Coastal Cellar in the Franschhoek Valley. The earlier winery, in Robertson, was a bold design combining strong colours and startling curved roofs; in Franschhoek, Wessels is just as forthright in his vision. He talks of building wineries from the inside out, and he contrives to make both aspects as striking as each other.

At this stage, I should make a confession. For some time now, I have developed a severe and debilitating aversion to bottling lines. I think I may be allergic to their monotonous hum and chink. Symptoms include vacuous staring and an overwhelming urge to hide inside a cardboard box. As far as possible, such areas are avoided. So when I hear that the main feature at Graham Beck Coastal Cellar is the building that houses the offices, art collection and – in pride of place – the bottling line, I am filled with trepidation. This had better be good.

Two shallow pools of water frame the façade, a dramatic piece of jutting stonework crafted from local stone by Angolan masons. Leopard sculptures prowl outside the entrance, a studded Moroccan door that leads into a soaring central space with ceiling clad in bleached Siberian pine. Inside, the geometric contortions of a flowing white sculpture take pride of place underneath sculpted white stairs. Glass is arranged inventively throughout the interior to give an almost weightless feel. And at the back, as the eye gradually attunes to the inside light, looms noiseless, insulated, almost a display piece behind its glass housing – the bottling line.

We had lunch overlooking the bottling line. It was a pleasure to behold the space that Wessels has

146 WINERIES WITH STYLE

Graham Beck Coastal Cellar SOUTH AFRICA >>145, 148

Graham Beck Coastal Cellar SOUTH AFRICA

created, with no attempt to conceal the industrial side of the winemaking process, instead combining it with lively architecture. His work generally defies labels, and at Graham Beck he has given the structure a vibrantly modern feel, yet also a noticeably African character. The doors, stonework, and sculptures all root the building in its continental African context – a feature that local architect-turned-winemaker David Trafford was later to compliment. "We don't do that enough in South Africa," he told me. It all has something of the character that one wine taster memorably described as "the sunshine taste".

Transforming the prosaic function of winemaking into poetic form is also a feature of Rymill, in Australia's celebrated Coonawarra region. It seems fitting that the direct descendants of the man who first established winemaking in Coonawarra in the 1890s should now be leading the charge in creating an iconic winery for the region.

Beauty in simplicity, a theme that runs through this chapter, is Rymill's hallmark. But behind the straightforward design lies a surprising range of influences. Architect Geoffrey Woodfall is frank in citing his references for the winery as thirteenth century French Gothic cathedrals, and such celebrated architects as Frank Lloyd Wright and Sir Norman Foster. But how, exactly, are such diverse influences incorporated into a highly functional winery? It's all in the honesty.

Woodfall took inspiration in the way these architects and structures make no bones about exposing what is termed the "structural fabric" of their buildings. In other words, there's no attempt at covering up what makes the buildings work, the basic building blocks. At Rymill, that open inspiration is given a very modern Australian feel in the triple gables, local materials, and brightly coloured pillars and beams. More importantly, though, it also unwraps the winemaking process.

Owner Peter Rymill was all for such transparency in the winery. "We designed it with viewing balconies on three levels, from which the visitors can see the winemakers in action, and feel they are part of the proceedings." The policy has evidently worked, as Rymill jokes "at vintage time, it is quite hard to get rid of them!" But the balconies don't just point inwards; in a clear echo of Frank Lloyd Wright's masterpiece house at Falling Water, Woodfall has extended balconies outside. One, a gravity-defying gangplank of a balcony, juts straight out from the winery's main façade, with views over the vineyards. The spaces flow into each other, opening up both the local region and the mechanics of making wine.

I asked Peter Rymill, a former international show jumper, why he went for such an architectural statement in his winery. "I think wine lovers are interested in where wine comes from," he answered. "I think there's a bit of the caveman in it. City dwellers have a subliminal urge to get out into the country; one way of doing that without leaving town is to indulge in a good bottle of wine. But it's better to do it properly."

Across the Tasman Sea in New Zealand, Sileni has the same sort of idea. Hawke's Bay is fast gaining recognition as an excellent wine-growing area, but the interest doesn't end there, as the likes of Sileni, Te Mata (*see* p.95), and Craggy Range (*see* p.138) demonstrate that wine can be enjoyed as part of a wider experience including food and architecture.

Sileni hints at the kind of dramatic, sweeping architecture we will be seeing in the next chapter, but here the concept is more rigorously functional. The brief was to keep the design simple, and architect George Paterson did just that, while also giving the winery a forceful character. The central hall is a case in point, the roof raised high to encapsulate the tall, stainless-steel tanks, and then

Graham Beck Coastal Cellar SOUTH AFRICA

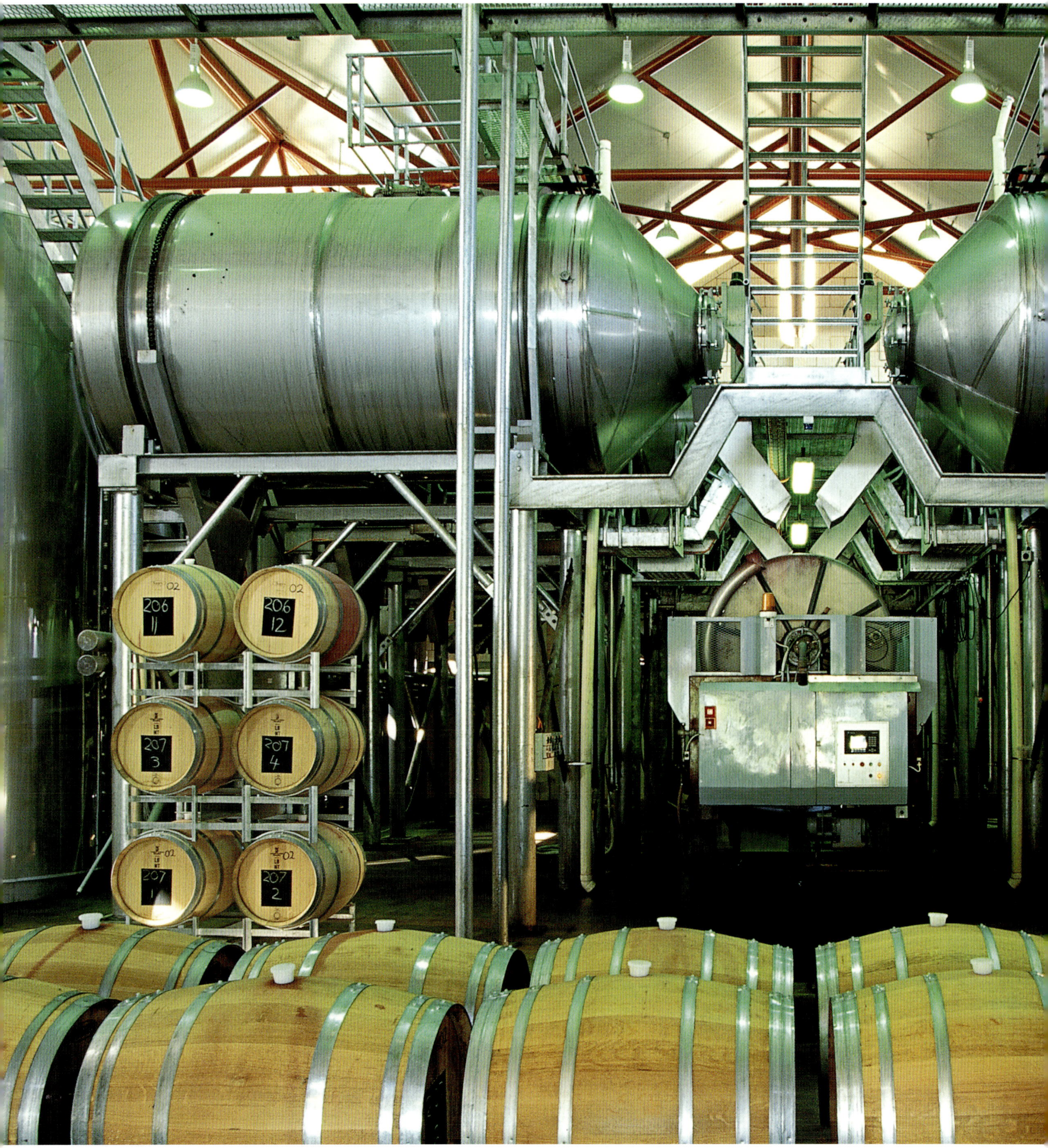
206
11
206
12
207
3
207
4
207
1
207
2

extended to project out over the entrance patio as a strong welcoming device and centrepiece for the winery's logo.

As at Rymill, Sileni's architects talk of how public participation in the winemaking operation was central to their design. It shows. Not just in the frank structure, but also in the additional elements like the pergola terraces, local river stones, and imaginative geometric forecourt that soften the industrial feel and create a sense of welcoming symmetry. Everything points to the way in. Sileni has an ambitious winemaking aim, to do for New Zealand reds what Cloudy Bay did for its whites. Its winery is a visual statement of that intent.

When the New World burst onto the modern international wine scene in the 1970s, many considered the likes of the USA, Chile, and Australia to be upstarts that would amount to little in terms of serious wine. They were wrong. And as the New World's wines have gained enduring recognition, so its confidence has been reflected in ambitious architectural statements in the wineries. Countries

IMMACULATE CONCEPTIONS

like Argentina, South Africa, and New Zealand are similar success stories. But there is one New World country, often overlooked, that has the longest winemaking tradition of the lot. And the odd winery to bring it to life.

Mexico has seen some magnificent civilizations in its time. With the arrival of Spanish colonists in the sixteenth century, the country's history took a dramatic new course, not least of which was the advent of vines, and a winemaking industry courtesy of the church. But it wasn't until the late nineteenth century that better vines were introduced to replace the rough missionary stock, and not until late in the twentieth century that serious wines were made from them.

Santo Tomás helped to pioneer that development. But it hasn't been easy, nor has this solemn, dusty landscape yet mounted a serious challenge on world markets. A cold Pacific ocean bullies Baja California's shoreline just south of the US border, where most of Mexico's wineries are located. Driving from the USA

Sileni NEW ZEALAND >>48, 151

translates manicured lawns into mangy dogs. I stop at the gas station; while we fill up I ask the pump attendants what they drink. "Beer and tequila, *señor*." "No wine?", I ask. They laugh heartily through the smell of petrol and fish, then shrug.

A few miles further on we arrive at Santo Tomás, a visible refutation of that indifference. The winery, in its imposing hilltop location, is a dramatic rendition of Mexico meets modernity. The steps of its stone walls recall Aztec temples, cacti speckle the base and rusted metal hues anchor the building in its landscape. Spidery metal spokes and reflective panels add a touch of surreal artistry. And yet Santo Tomás is more than architectural frippery – its form stems largely from an ingenious practical arrangement.

Gravity. While the concept of gravity flow is common to a number of wineries in this book, rarely is it enshrined in such style as at Santo Tomás. The idea is simple – instead of using energy and money pumping wine all around your

Sileni NEW ZEALAND

IMMACULATE CONCEPTIONS   153

Santo Tomás MEXICO >>152–3, 155

winery, let gravity do the work. At Santo Tomás, you can drive onto the roof – because the rooftop also doubles up as a reception area where grapes are off-loaded at harvest. Convenient hatches provide access into the winery and its tanks. The occasion must be like a sacrificial ritual atop such a carefully contrived, almost ceremonial structure. From the tanks, the wine flows into the barrel cellars, reached by tunnels that would not look out of place in a submarine. The transformation is complete.

Owner Santiago Cosío describes it as a "soft and easy operation", which "uses gravity as a friend". Just how far the winery does descend into the hill is made plain by a series of mesmerizing spiral staircases that run down the winery's side and into the earth. Going down seems fine; coming up is another matter. The priorities seem to be clear – while the wine gets an easy ride, the winemakers are kept firmly in shape.

If this is indeed the case, then the personnel at Malivoire in Canada must be just as lithe as those at Santo Tomás. On the other side of the great American interlude, Ontario is often more ice wine than spicy enchilada in its climate, but the gravity concept at Malivoire is remarkably similar to that at the Mexican winery. All that's different – and it's quite a big difference – is the shape of the winery.

Instead of burrowing into a hilltop, owner Martin Malivoire decided to take advantage of a nine-metre (thirty-foot) ravine in a newly acquired vineyard to build his winery. A corrugated iron hut on the property gave him the inspiration for a ribbed metal shell – its appearance reminded him of vineyard rows on a hillside. And so the Malivoire winery was born, a curious and unassuming steel shell that careers down its ravine-side. Malivoire was so fanatical about realizing his concept that architect Andrew Vogyesi reportedly joked that he was only there as "window dressing".

Inside, winemaking is carried out on no less than seven levels. Malivoire wanted a gravity-concept winery for a number of reasons. Principally, to promote careful treatment of the grapes, and to avoid extraction of unwanted bitterness that can result from harsh mechanical action on the juice and wine. His winemaker Ann Sperling was also keen on the design as an ideal way to make Pinot Noir, a tricky grape at the best of times. "Our winery was built the way it was built so we can make wine the way we want to make wine," is the company's admirably simple line.

There have been concessions, though. For example, Malivoire's original design was gravity-propelled austerity itself, but a public area was later incorporated with more homely touches. Some pumping is now carried out, too – Malivoire describes his adherence to all things gravity as having evolved from "fanatical" to "dedicated". Nonetheless, the winery retains its distinctive down-to-earth appeal.

Malivoire CANADA

Haras de Pirque CHILE >>159

Haras de Pirque CHILE

Shy and retiring, however, is hardly the way to describe Haras de Pirque. Perhaps the most ambitious of the three gravity-concept wineries featured here, Haras is situated on the lower slopes of the Andes foothills in central Chile. Why so audacious, you might ask? Haras is both a horse stud and vineyard. And the winery, built commandingly into the hillside, is in the shape of a horseshoe.

"This is a nice story behind the wines – fine horses and fine wines are a phenomenal combination. What do you think?" asks an enthused Eduardo Matte. It certainly is an original take on the winemaking process – rarely have I been conveyed to a winery in horse and vintage carriage after casting my eye over several prize stallions. Approaching the winery, it appears solid and daunting, with what appears to be a pyramid-like shape in the centre.

But Haras isn't just about the novelty factor. In fact, the horseshoe, or omega, shape is only readily apparent when looking down on the winery from above. And you soon realize that the supposed pyramid shape is merely an optical illusion – these are just steps in an open central courtyard. The hillside location serves as the ideal site for a gravity-induced winemaking process, as the wine flows down through each wing, finally ending up in the sunken central barrel cellar.

The winery's hillside site is also something of a statement in terms of viticultural intent. Around eighty per cent of Haras' vineyards are planted on slopes. In Chile, the ongoing search for real quality and a sense of Chilean identity in the wines means producers are increasingly planting on such gradients. The idea is that by giving the vines poorer, shallower soils and better light exposure, the wines are correspondingly more complex and expressive than the sort of juicy fruit produced from flat, fertile vineyard land, of which much exists in Chile. Chilean wine, Haras proclaims, should head for the hills.

IMMACULATE CONCEPTIONS

IN BRIEF

VINA REAL
Rioja, Spain
BUILT 2004 by Philippe Mazières
WINE TIP Viña Real Blanco Fermentado en Barrica
VISITS By appointment
www.cvne.com

Viña Real used to be nothing more than a label made by the large, though top-notch, CVNE operation. Now it has its very own, very impressive, winery. Wines are excellent.

LOUIS JADOT LA SABLIERE
Beaune, Burgundy, France
BUILT 1997 by Cabinet Seturec
WINE TIP Gevrey-Chambertin Les Cazetiers
VISITS By appointment
www.louisjadot.com

Burgundy can be an erratic enigma in wine terms, so it's comforting to have a large winemaker producing consistently excellent wines. La Sablière helps in this task and adds a touch of razzmatazz to proceedings.

CRAGGY RANGE
Hawke's Bay, New Zealand
BUILT 2002 by John Blair
WINE TIP Gimblett Gravels Merlot
VISITS Open doors
www.craggyrange.com

When the owners came to look around, they thought "Craggy Range" was a great name for a winery. Up it went and now some impressive single-vineyard wines are also doing their bit for the winery's good name.

TERRE DA VINO
Barolo, Piedmont, Italy
BUILT 2000 by Gianni Arnaudo
WINE TIP Croere Barbera d'Alba
VISITS Open doors
www.terredavino.it

What a find – large co-ops in remote, hilly areas are usually allergic to the first hint of innovation, but this one has really taken the plunge. Wines can be hit and miss but some are lovely.

RANSOM
Matakana, Auckland, New Zealand
BUILT 2001 by Graeme Scott
WINE TIP Clos de Valerie Pinot Gris
VISITS Open doors
www.matakanawine.com

The new wave of southern hemisphere winemaking has acted like a wake-up call to the traditionally Eurocentric wine world. Ransom is doing its bit for New Zealand's winemaking identity. Good on them.

CHATEAU HAUT SELVE
Graves, Bordeaux, France
BUILT 1996 by Sylvain Dubuisson
WINE TIP 2000 vintage (red)
VISITS By appointment
www.chateau-branda.com

Bordeaux is not as tied to tradition as you might think – Haut Selve is visible proof of the fact. It still aims to express the time-honoured character of its Graves terroir, though.

DORNIER
Helderberg, Stellenbosch, South Africa
BUILT 2003 by Johan Malherbe
WINE TIP Donatus white
VISITS Open doors
www.dornierwines.co.za

A modern South African winery owned by Swiss-based artist Christoph Dornier. It was always going to be something special. The wines look promising – the first vintage was 2002.

160 WINERIES WITH STYLE

STAATSWEINGUT WEINSBERG
Württemberg, Germany
BUILT 2002 by Hugo Mattes
WINE TIP Riesling Trocken
VISITS Open doors
www.lvwo.bwl.de

Why didn't my parents send me to a school filled with wine? Weinsberg is both a wine college and wine-producer. It may feel at times like a classroom, but what a classroom.

GRAHAM BECK COASTAL CELLAR
Franschhoek, South Africa
BUILT 2002 by Johan Wessels
WINE TIP The Ridge Shiraz
VISITS By appointment
www.grahambeckwines.co.za

Graham Beck has two wineries – one at Madeba in Robertson, the other nearer the coast in Franschhoek. Both are worth a peek in their own right, for wines as well as architecture.

RYMILL
Coonawarra, Australia
BUILT 1990 by Geoffrey Woodfall
WINE TIP mc^2
VISITS Open doors
www.rymill.com.au

Few Australian wineries bring as much history to the table as Rymill, whose origins in the highly regarded Coonawarra region date back to the 1890s. You wouldn't have guessed it from this modern marvel. All wines come highly recommended.

SILENI
Hawke's Bay, New Zealand
BUILT 1999 by Dodd Paterson & Bukowski Rehm
WINE TIP The Circle Semillon
VISITS Open doors
www.sileni.co.nz

For a relatively simple structure, Sileni doesn't lack for much, with two restaurants, offices, a culinary school, food store, and wine education centre rubbing shoulders with the winemaking.

SANTO TOMAS
Ensenada, Baja California, Mexico
BUILT 1995 by Alejandro d'Acosta
WINE TIP Barbera
VISITS By appointment
www.santo-tomas.com

From one of the New World's most historic but least-known winemaking countries comes this gem of a winery. Modern winemaking is given a Mexican makeover. What better winery to champion the country's winemaking cause?

MALIVOIRE
Niagara Peninsula, Ontario, Canada
BUILT 1998 by Volgyesi & Propst
WINE TIP Moira Vineyard Gewürztraminer
VISITS By appointment
www.malivoire.com

Homespun winemaking is the order of the day at Malivoire, and a very effective version of it, too. Gravity is the key on this ravine-side winery – up to seven levels are used.

HARAS DE PIRQUE
Pirque, Maipo, Chile
BUILT 2000 by Jaime Burgos
WINE TIP Haras Character Cabernet Sauvignon
VISITS By appointment
www.harasdepirque.com

A winery shaped like a horseshoe? The estate includes a horse stud; the horseshoe shape allows for an effective gravity-flow winemaking process. The wines aren't bad, either. It all makes sense.

Malivoire CANADA

Haras de Pirque CHILE

Rymill AUSTRALIA

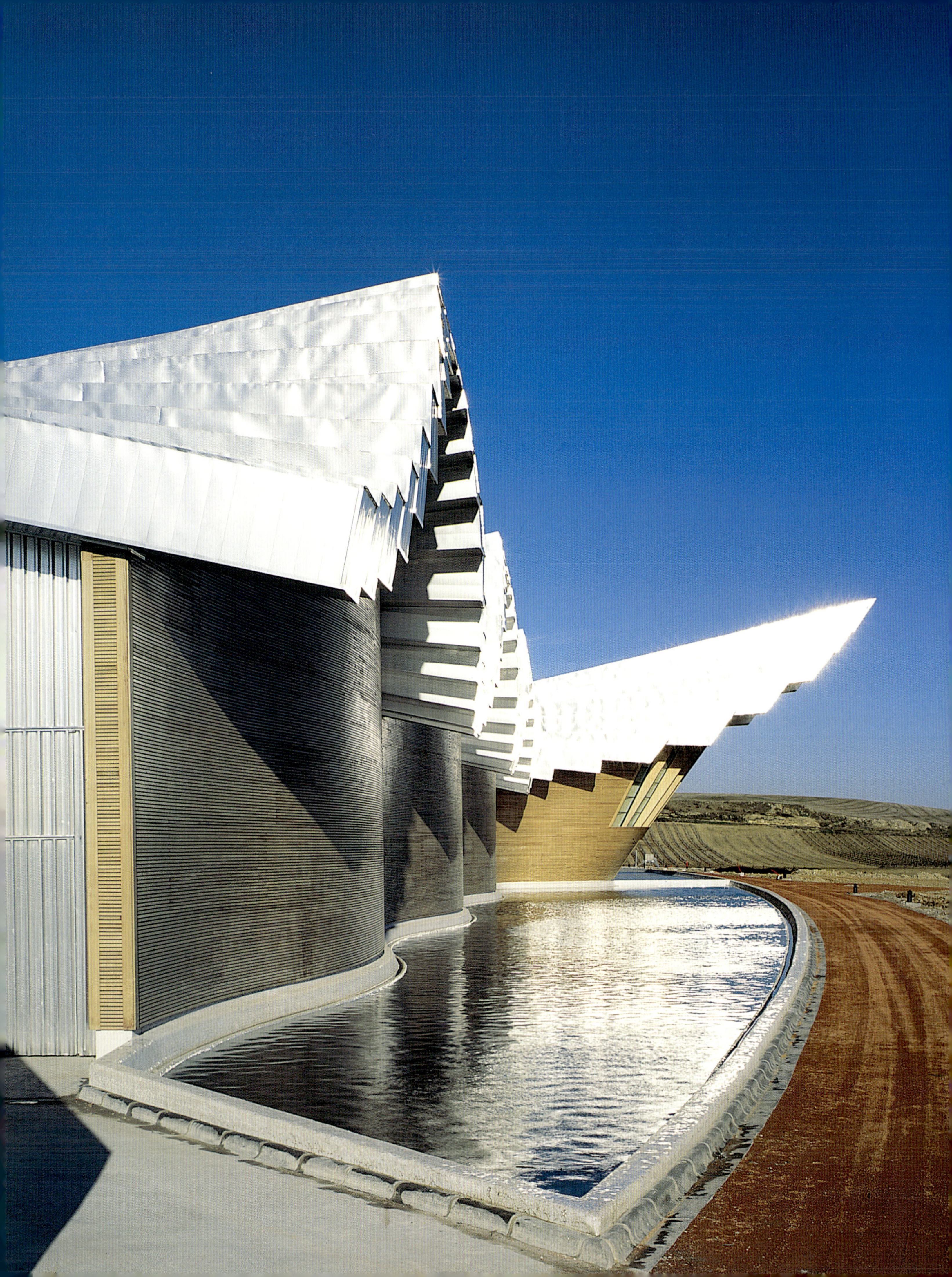

A NEW WORLD

A STYLISH FUTURE FOR WINE

"Since our life must at the best be but a vapour that appears for a little time and then vanishes away, let it at least appear as a cloud in the height of Heaven, not as the thick darkness that broods over the blast of the Furnace." Victorian architecture critic and wine merchant's son, John Ruskin.

Ysios SPAIN

A thunderstorm is brewing. Around us, huge towers of white cloud shepherd our plane towards the land, their shadows firm like pedestals on the granite waters of Biscay below. They are oddly comforting.

But ahead, over land, a troubling dark wall of cloud awaits the plane. Few people are talking now; faces are turned to windows. It is left to a baby to voice our unease, but even its cries are smothered by the oppressive atmosphere as we fly into the storm. Flashes of lightning vanish as soon as they come, distant for now, but furtive. We cross from sea to land and immediately the plane begins to be jostled and buffeted by a spitting, liquid landscape. We bank for our run into Bilbao.

The simple act of walking comes as a huge release after such a landing. This isn't the first time I've had such a reception at Bilbao – I begin to wonder if it's not coincidence. It's as if the Basque Country, this rugged, untamed corner of northern Spain, likes to give its own brand of fiery welcome to the visitor.

To add fuel to that fire, the impression is not just given by the turbulent weather at Bilbao airport – it's there in concrete, steel, and glass, too. Spanish architect, artist, and engineer, Santiago Calatrava's breathtaking airport building has all the movement and dynamism of the planes that service it, its scything, jutting white form reminiscent, as many of Calatrava's buildings, of a giant prehistoric creature plunging through the elements.

A few miles down the road is a more recognizable building. The swirling metal folds of Frank Gehry's Guggenheim Museum have done wonders for Bilbao's image, helping to transform this largely industrial town into a thriving cultural centre. It radiates a sense of excitement and controversy – love it or hate it, it's nigh on impossible to ignore it.

Calatrava and Gehry are two of the most exhilarating, original, and visionary architects of our times. Their influence is global, their work iconic. Bilbao is a good example of how such challenging architecture can revive an entire region. So the fact that both Gehry and Calatrava, not to mention many other top architects, are now weaving their magic on wineries is hugely exciting. It is a celebration of a whole new world of wine.

Bilbao is the gateway to Rioja. What is already Spain's most famous wine-growing region is now transforming itself into one of the global hotspots for landmark wineries, as stunning constructions continue to rise amid the windy slopes of this wide valley. As one Riojan said to me, slightly tongue in cheek, "Rioja has the tradition of Bordeaux but the architecture of Napa." Ysios, designed by Calatrava, is one of its highlights.

What struck me most about Ysios when I visited was just how well the winery sits in the landscape. To look at the fierce undulations of its gleaming roof, it seems just too futuristic, too dramatic to blend with nature. And yet Calatrava is a firm believer in the fact that structures should relate to their surroundings. He describes Ysios as "both an architectural landmark and an element completely integrated in its surroundings."

This is quite a claim to make and yet his words do ring true. The aluminum-clad roof reflects the grey crags of the Cantabrian Mountains behind; the golden cedar-wood façade is the colour of the wheat fields and light soils of Rioja. It's also interesting to note what Calatrava means in terms of surroundings. "A landscape should never be seen as static. Something dynamic is always happening. As soon as the wind blows, the trees will move. The sun moves. The shadows and clouds move… I recognize this dynamic aspect of the landscape," he writes, "and feel compelled to express it in my work."

Dynamic is a good word for Ysios. Perhaps the building's most affecting moment comes inside the craning expanse of its central projection, looking out from under monumental forty-two-metre (135-foot) Scandinavian fir beams towards the medieval village of Laguardia. Rioja is stuffed full of history and tradition (not just in terms of wine: prehistoric and

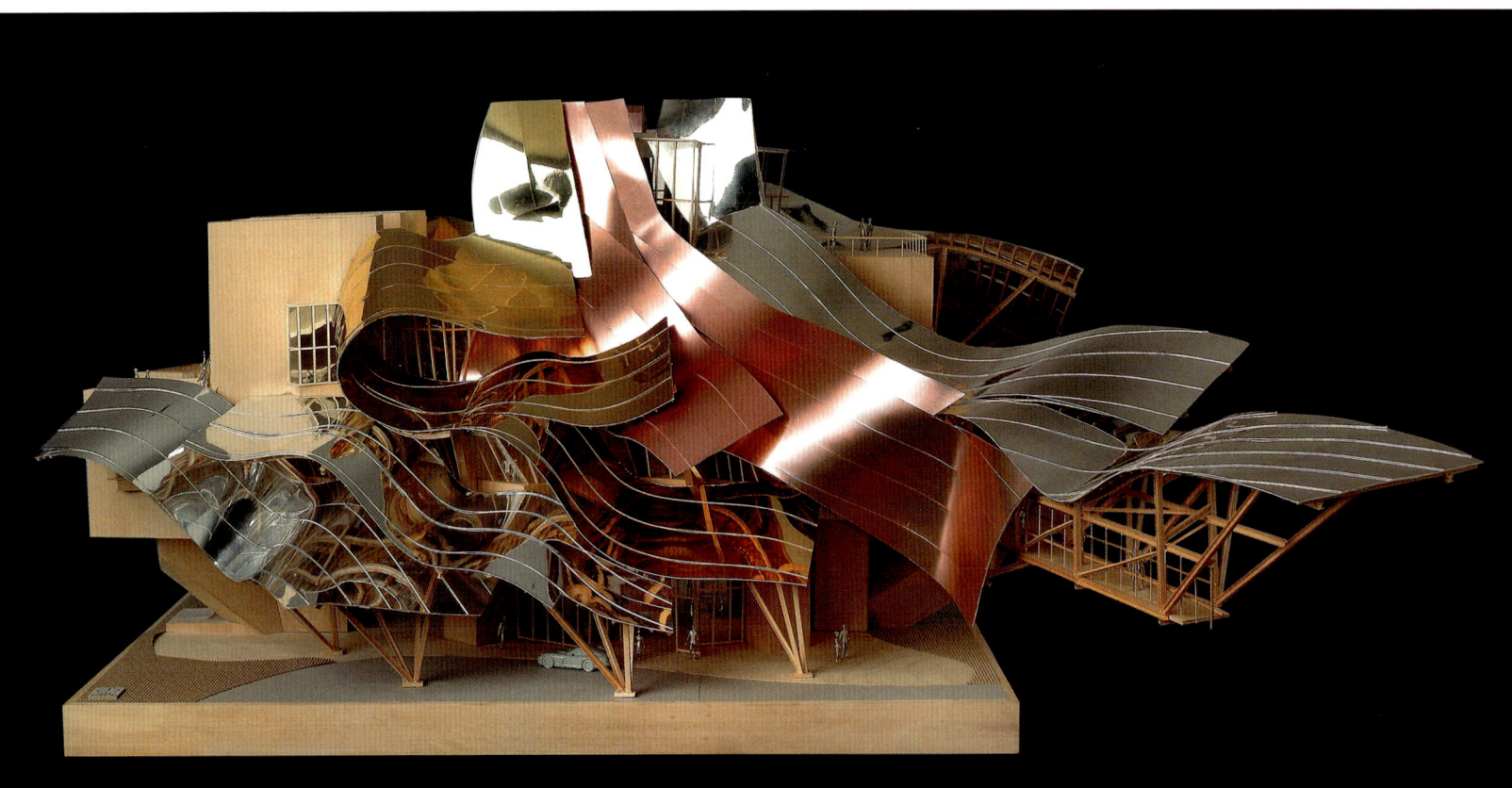

Roman remains also lie nearby) but Ysios transforms this legacy into a vibrant, modern winery. It's the kind of winery that is forcibly dragging, not just Rioja, but the entire wine world into the future in some style.

It's interesting to note that the winery itself is a fairly simple construct. A linear process running from west to east, the winemaker with his steel tanks and wooden barrels is at the peaceful eye of this architectural storm. Even the wave-like roof is a relatively uncomplicated interplay of straight beams tilted across two parallel concrete walls – a long-time sculptural theme of Calatrava's. From straight lines he has created curves and movement; simplicity made grandeur.

There is no doubt that Ysios is raising the profile of wine. It's alluring, challenging, and presents an image that is readily associated with a modern wine industry. But it is not alone in that endeavour. In the nearby village of Elciego, the historic estate of Marqués de Riscal has secured the talents of superstar architect Frank Gehry to stake its claim.

Gehry is one of architecture's most prominent figures and his buildings tend to be just as recognizable. Riscal, meanwhile, is known for being one of Rioja's oldest producers, yet also one of its more consistently innovative. Gehry's creation, the Bilbao Guggenheim, paved the way for a startling new structure at the heart of Riscal's sprawling historic premises in Elciego, parts of which date back to 1860. As in Bilbao, this was to be a radical revamp. (Gehry was reportedly courted with bottles of the vintage from his birth year, 1929.)

The new building is to act as an iconic presence at Riscal, though not as a winery. It's the wine estate concept, known best from its manifestations in Bordeaux châteaux (such as Margaux, *see* p.20) in which it is a collection of buildings and not a single structure that make up the winemaking property. This is strangely apt for Riscal, whose original nineteenth-century architecture was copied from Bordeaux estates just as its pioneering winemaking model came directly from French influence.

Gehry's own drastic brand of wine château is a typically convoluted mass of metallic roofing over a series of box-shaped stone rooms and glass walls. The coloured titanium roofing in pink, silver, and gold is designed to echo motifs found in wine bottles. Its seemingly chaotic – actually carefully computer-designed – contortions are as mesmerizing as they are daring.

The one question mark that hangs over the new Riscal development is how well it will fit into and age within its decidedly rural context. The building is taller than it might seem and when finished in 2005 is planned to stop a scarcely deferential two metres (six-and-a-half feet) short of the parish church spire. Is this just too much modernity for a dusty country village? Time will tell. Riscal hopes it will bring the area and their winery to life, attracting wine and architecture lovers alike. As Gehry said, "I want buildings that have passion in them, that have feeling in them, that make people feel something, even if they get mad at them."

It's hard to get angry; I think it's a revelation. Worried I was getting a little carried away with myself, though, I badgered my sister Helen, an architect based in New Zealand, for her views on Gehry and Calatrava. She was on my side. "Functional buildings are great in their practicality, but we want more than that! Gehry and Calatrava stand out like beacons due to the way in which they push boundaries, creating exhilarating and uplifting architecture, an elevation of the senses. They may be the epitome of luxury but they are also inventors of inspiration." One of Gehry's self-stated aims is for architecture "to make a difference, to enlighten, and to enrich the human experience."

Such a view no doubt finds strong support in the world of fine wine, which has similar aims. It comes as no surprise, then, to find that Gehry is also working on another wine project, though this time in his native Canada. Le Clos Jordanne is a project for a winery and vineyard on the Niagara Peninsula, a joint-venture between Canada's Vincor and Burgundy-based Boisset. Unlike Riscal, this building will be a working winery, while still retaining Gehry's trademark style.

Though it is not scheduled for completion until at least 2007, Le Clos Jordanne is already making its name, in wine circles and beyond. The angular white walls and flowing metallic roof are classic Gehry, the interior ordered around one cavernous hall that affords a panoramic view of the winemaking process. As Gehry commented at the project's launch: "the making of the wine will seem like part of the architectural experience."

The architect describes the winery as, alternatively, a landscape, a blanket, and a cloud. This is typical of Gehry, breaking down traditional shapes and materials into fluid forms. In a light-hearted touch, one proposal currently under consideration is to have wine-like liquid flowing inside monumental transparent columns stretching from cellar to roof. This is not all play, though, as Gehry makes clear. "It was important to us that it not just be a fancy building that had nothing to do with the people, it had to speak with the vineyard, it had to speak to wine production… the energy of the building is not only in the architecture, it is in the energy of making wine."

Marqués de Riscal SPAIN

In the introduction I mentioned Spanish architect Jesús Marino Pascual, who spoke of how we are living through a change of era. Although our discussion was about wine and architecture in general, he later went on to identify what is driving this change in architecture specifically. Computer-aided design. Calatrava uses it. Gehry uses it, with bells on – his CATIA system is the same set-up used to design Mirage fighter jets. Marino has designed three Spanish wineries that are to be built over the coming years: Darien, Irius, and Antion. "I couldn't have designed them without this kind of technology," he says.

Since ancient times, architects have worked in two dimensions, Marino explains. Now, with the advent of computer technology, it's possible to work in three dimensions. "It enables us to understand space in ways that were previously impossible," he enthuses. "We can now design buildings that we could only have dreamed of doing twenty years ago. It helps us understand the viability of structures." In other words, architects can now be more daring than they ever have been in the history of architecture.

Gehry and Calatrava's buildings are two examples of such bold new architecture and, when Marino's wineries are complete, they look set to join the exalted cast. Irius, for example, is championed by the breathless promotional literature as "a global reference for technological advance in the wine industry – an unmissable experience for those restless souls who seek the image of tomorrow today." When I went to interview José Luis Lázaro, president of Proconsol, the group behind Irius and Antion, he was so excited that I could hardly get away. As I escaped into the night, I could still hear him chattering after me: "this is the future of wine!"

Both Irius and Antion are ambitious projects. For Antion, Marino had to squeeze a complex structure, including a hotel and restaurant as well as the winery, into an awkwardly shaped plot of land. Space was tight as the land either side does not belong to them. Large parts of the winery are underground, but the main structure works around a circular vinification centre, fanning out like a whip into hotel rooms. Flowing shapes throw shadows to create an atmospheric working interior.

Antion's compact, landscaped nature contrasts with the sheer size and scale of Irius. It's easier to see with Irius how computer-aided design has played a part in its creation – the complex geometry of colliding volumes is startling. Silver skin and blue-tinted windows give an impression of steely modernity. As for its jumbled shape, Marino describes it as "reflecting the Pyrénées Mountains, just like the pool of water reflects the winery."

There was more space and freedom to work with at Irius. Somontano is far removed from the smallholdings and stifling tradition of Rioja. Amid these immense dusty plains at the foot of the Pyrénées, Irius will sit at the centre of a radiating spider's web of vineyards. "It's a twenty-first-century winery and vineyard," says Lázaro.

Like at Antion, the key sections of the winery at Irius are underground. This is a hallmark of Marino's winery architecture – concealing the main production centres underground while linking them to the more architecturally adventurous public parts of the winery. The effect of transparency is not weakened, as the design allows for visitors to see into all of the production areas from the main gallery. In addition, the winemaking process benefits from temperature insulation and natural light from carefully placed and craftily designed skylights.

"We wanted the wine to remain as undisturbed as possible during its elaboration," explains Marino with regard to Darien, which shares the same basic design pattern as Irius. "The question was, how to link the social part of the winery to the production part with as little interference as possible?" The answer was glass, which forms an integral part of both designs, allowing light in and open views throughout the buildings. "You'll even be able to eat overlooking the winemaking if you want," smiles Marino.

Unlike Irius, Darien's environment is characterized by slopes, undulations, rocky outcrops, layered stone, – and the tradition of Rioja. Marino found an ingenious solution. He applied the same kind of adventurous geometric design evident at Irius, but on this occasion modelled his structure very carefully on the specific kind of layered, rocky outcrops visible throughout the surrounding area. The idea was to pay homage to tradition and nature, but make no concessions to modernity. "The building will be grey-white concrete," says Marino. "Raw concrete has a sincere and strong character; it should not be clad or covered. It needs no make-up."

Marino also talks about sustainability in his wine architecture. This is a key point that is not often given the time it merits in wineries. A few weeks earlier, I had spoken to Roger Boulton, eminent winemaking professor at UC Davis in California. He was scathing in his assessment of winery design, saying that all too often, the right questions concerning environmental efficiency are simply not addressed at the design stage.

Boulton's point is that wineries can be enormously wasteful in terms of water and energy, but there is no need for this to be the case with adequate information, sharing, and forward planning. "The wine industry has a great opportunity to pioneer eco-friendly architecture and get the kudos for it," runs his argument. Marino agrees. "All architecture should aim for sustainability," he says, "especially in the wine industry." In other words, priority should be given to environmental ends, just as much as other design considerations.

The advances of technology that are enabling ever-more futuristic wineries to be built have also contributed to a revolution in wine terms. Technology, such as temperature-controlled, stainless steel has been a huge step forward in producing clean, fresh wines in hot climates. And yet, for all the technological advances, wine often likes to retain an aura of tradition, earthiness, and, sometimes, even anonymity.

It was a defining moment in 1997 when Swiss architects Herzog and de Meuron put the finishing touches to the inscrutable stone box that is the Dominus winery in Napa Valley. They had been commissioned by owner Christian Moueix, also administrator of the stellar Bordeaux wine producer (though architecturally modest) Château Pétrus. The brief was to design a winery that was both practical and pioneering, but far from attention-seeking.

An invisible winery? The likes of Artesa (*see* p.53) come close, but as far as above-ground structures go, Dominus tackles the challenge in totally original style. The functional concrete structure is clad in loose chunks of basalt rock, held together by steel mesh baskets known as gabions and more commonly found on roadsides. The locally quarried rocks are a mix of natural green, black, and grey colours and increase in size towards the top of the building, allowing more light through, the idea being that the structure appears to dissolve into the air. Apart from camouflaging the winery, the rocks also provide effective thermal insulation and lend the building an earthy, agricultural sense of purpose. It all seems so simple and yet so inventive.

172 WINERIES WITH STYLE

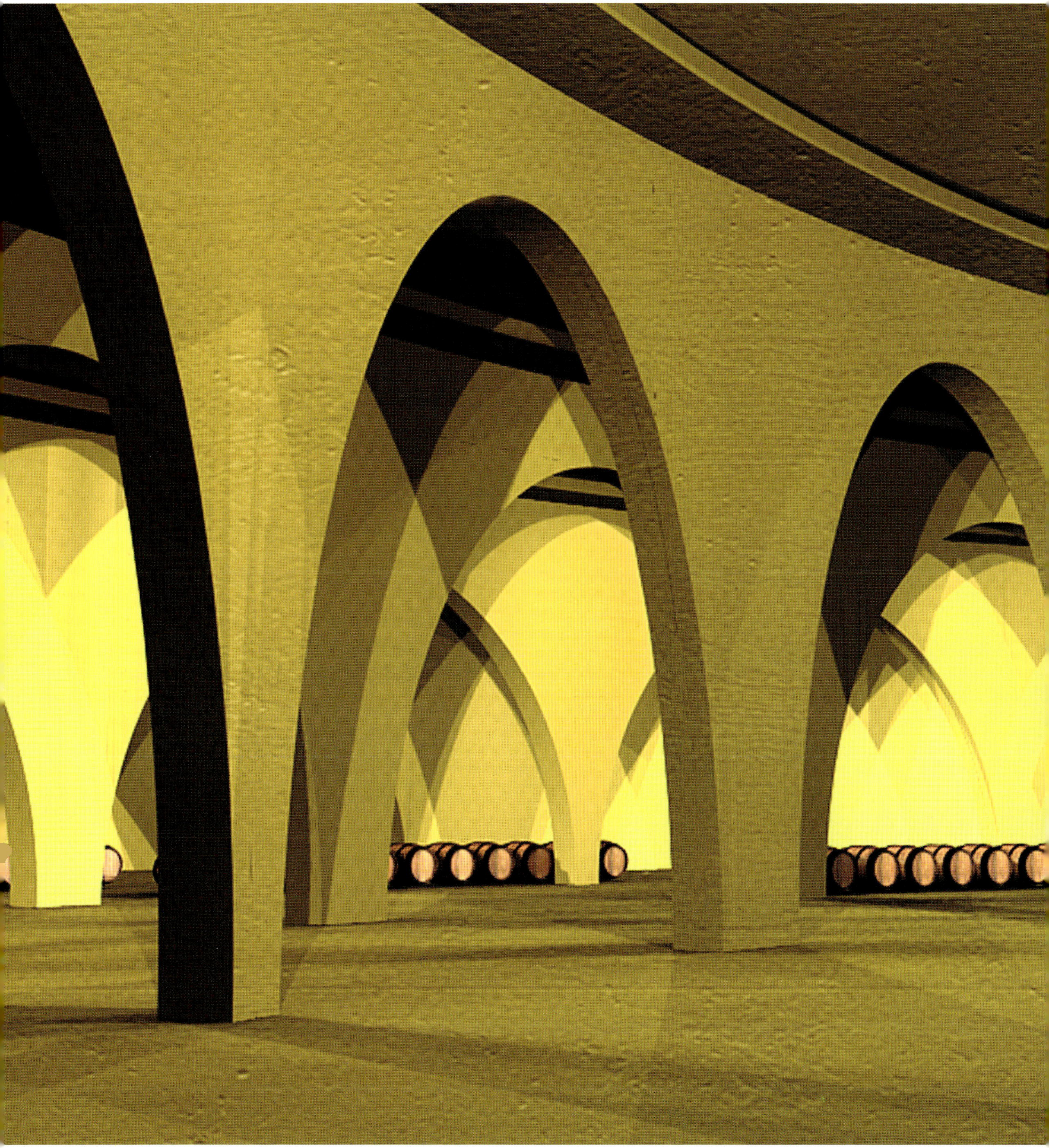

Darien SPAIN >>170

The idea of invisibility at Dominus is to put the emphasis on the vines, not the winery. When I visited, I got the feeling that there was a reticence to discuss the winery without first discussing the vineyard in depth. "It's the same reason why we don't accept visits by the public," says Boris. "It's not arrogance, it's common sense. We have one focus: the wine. We won't be distracted from that."

Nonetheless, Dominus is full of contradictions. It's almost monastic in its simplicity, yet is packed with the features of great architecture. It shuns attention, but is an attraction in its own right. Most importantly, however, it's an efficient winery in which excellent wine is made. Its true value is in having ripped up the rulebook of winery design and started a fresh new chapter.

Starting afresh was something that Hungary had to do in the 1990s after decades of neglect and poor management under communist rule. Disznókő, a traditional wine estate in the Tokaji region, rose to the challenge in style after it was bought by French insurance group AXA. Architect Dezsö Ekler was brought in and the estate underwent a rapid renaissance in 1992.

What's enjoyable about Disznókő is the way it confounds stereotypes. "Hungary?" you might ask. Hardly cutting edge. And you'd be wrong to dismiss it so hastily. Ekler's architecture is tricky to pin down. In the winery, he adds a fresh and light feel to winemaking practicality in his original bent spine arrangement. But the centrepiece is surely the humble tractor-shed, which has been transformed into a monumental yawning structure with curious spikes, a hollow core and furled roof. Its warm timber struts are reminiscent of those in the winery's main gallery. At Disznókő they've dubbed it, "Probably the prettiest tractor shed in the world."

Tokaji has for centuries enjoyed considerable renown for its sweet wines, the best of which have traditionally been aged in dank cellars for considerable amounts of time. Disznókő takes a modern approach, both in its winemaking and winery, with traditional cellars dug ten metres (thirty-three feet) into the rock, but crowned with a winery that embraces thoroughly modern methods and design. Its presence has played a significant part in Tokaji's re-emergence into the modern era.

It was raining a light, persistent drizzle when I walked up the long driveway to the low-slung winery. Clouds crept down the hillside vineyard behind as I talked to winemaker Boris Champy. While we tasted, rain drummed softly against the skylight and spattered off the rocks and steel cages outside. Aromas of fresh rain and wet earth slipped through the building. The wines smelled of olives, fresh fruit, and dried leaves. As I left, I turned to check if the theory of invisible architecture held water. Dominus certainly wasn't invisible, any more than it wasn't a serious wine producer. But if you hadn't taken the time to look, you might never have known it was there.

AXA had also been active elsewhere in the world of wine and architecture, having commissioned imaginative new winemaking facilities at Château Pichon-Longueville Baron in Bordeaux (see p.75). The architects for that job were Patrick Dillon and Jean de Gastines, who later went on to design a new winery in a dramatic hilltop location in South Africa. Its name was Vergelegen.

WINERIES WITH STYLE

Dominus USA >>171, 174

Dominus USA

Dominus USA

The architects were chosen precisely for their ability to work sensitively around existing historical edifices as they had done at Pichon. Vergelegen's past came in the form of an immaculate collection of Cape Dutch houses, with typical whitewashed walls and gables under thatched roofing, as well as an octagonal rose garden dating back to the early 1700s. The brief was to create a winery on an octagonal plan that would blend into its environment and afford spectacular views over the valley, mountains, and False Bay. Not only that, it should also be strikingly original and respect criteria outlined by winemaker at the time, Martin Meinert.

It's interesting to see some of the architects' original designs for the winery, with scribbled notes providing an insight into the creative process. One reads: "we're going to make the most impeccable state-of-the-art winery in Africa and top it off with a temple to Venus." Another: "architecture here should be essential, and yet embody the poetry of the land, this would be the best homage to Cape Dutch." Meinert relates how he wanted to retain "a Cape aesthetic", but with "a freshness that, hopefully, would set new standards". The aim was no less than "to break new architectural ground".

Standing on top of Vergelegen's commanding position, with a stiff breeze whipping over the winery's crisp white lines, you can't help but feel they succeeded. Much of the structure (three of the four levels) is sunk into the hill to take advantage of gravity in the vinification process, but on top, like a determined periscope, is a ridged white box with glass panels. This is the entry point, from which a spiral staircase descends into a more circular, vertical winemaking world. It retains a distinct Cape Dutch feel, yet is fresh as well as functional – albeit hard work for the winery staff who have to negotiate all those stairs.

Paying tribute to the landscape is done in very different but equally innovative fashion at Mezzacorona in Italy's northern Trentino valley. Here, the narrow valley floor is hemmed in on either side by the towering grey walls of the Dolomites as they rise to meet the Alps and Austria. It is a landscape of viticultural opportunism, with vines clinging to impossibly steep slopes as well as enjoying the odd flat expanse of valley floor where the mountains briefly widen. One such enclave is the Rotaliano plain, and it is here that Mezzacorona decided to build a new base in 1995.

Despite the narrow confines of its valley, Mezzacorona is a huge operation. As a cooperative cellar it receives fruit from around 2,400 hectares (almost 6,000 acres) and 1,300 wine-growers. When architect Alberto Cecchetto was tasked to design a correspondingly ambitious new winery on an abandoned industrial site, there was one main condition: respect the surroundings. They had chosen the right man – Cecchetto is a fierce exponent of what he terms "architecture that grows out of its setting". With Mezzacorona, the challenge was on an industrial-sized scale.

Harvest time is a spectacle of epic industry at Mezzacorona. Weary, weathered growers pour through the gates, their trailers overflowing with grapes, anxious at the quality check station, expeditious at the reception hoppers. It's a bustling interaction between the chaotic,

A NEW WORLD

colourful movements of nature on the one hand, and the clinical industry of the winemaking process on the other. This is just what Cecchetto was looking to express in the architecture of Mezzacorona.

The local pergola system for training the vines was the model for the undulating roof. Its supporting pillars represent the stakes; the transparent strips allow light to filter through as if in a canopy between two adjacent vines. Inside, the natural light and curvy, warm wood lend a breezy feel to the industry. Outside, the metallic greys and silvers of the structure pick up on the colours of the stern mountains behind. The mixture of artistry and industry reflects the blend of Italian ebullience and Austrian efficiency that is characteristic of this frontier region.

The company have dubbed this project La Cittadella del Vino. Its scale warrants such a title, with three massive facilities spread over a twelve-hectare site. Apart from purely practical concerns, the aim, I was told, is to "make a

Disznókő HUNGARY

Vergelegen SOUTH AFRICA >>174, 177

splash in the world of wine". What's good about Mezzacorona is that its scale and ambitions have not divorced it from the local surroundings – instead Cecchetto has made value out of the union between the two.

A penchant for undulating roofs in mountain locations is a feature that Mezzacorona shares with Chile's Almaviva. Aside from the fact that both wineries are inspired modern reflections of their environments, however, their similarity ends there. The Almaviva winery is devoted to making just one wine, and that only in modest quantities. It is a prestigious joint-venture between Chilean winemaking giant Concha y Toro and the Rothschilds of Bordeaux's Mouton-Rothschild (they of the iconic Californian collaboration Opus One [see p.114–21]). Almaviva is about exclusivity, luxury, and the union of two winemaking cultures.

Chile is a captivating country. Its waiflike form runs thousands of kilometres from polar icecaps to scorching desert, all the while shadowed by Andean peaks on one side and the Pacific Ocean on the other. Its history speaks of indigenous

180   WINERIES WITH STYLE

Mapuche tribes and Spanish conquistadors; its richness has long been measured in forests, mining, fish, fruit, and wine. Architect Martín Hurtado's winery for Almaviva would have to reflect all of that as well as incorporating a sense of French refinement. "So, we thought, how do we show the world what a Chilean winemaking facility is like? What are we identified with?" Hurtado's answer was: "geography and nature. A wine of great standing has to show its place of origin, its terroir, and this (winery) is no exception."

The undulating roof unifies the four winemaking units, but it is also a brilliant creative touch that mimics the peaks of the nearby Andes. Wood is used extensively in the structure – evocatively-named Chilean woods like *coïhue, lingue, raulí* – in fact, all the winery's doors are made from old *raulí* wine vats recycled from Concha y Toro. "Geography and nature – mountains and forests," muses Hurtado.

But the drive for Chilean identity doesn't end there. Works of art dotted throughout the winery make vivid reference to the country's indigenous cultures.

Mezzacorona ITALY

A NEW WORLD

WINERIES WITH STYLE

Mezzacorona ITALY >>177–180

Almaviva CHILE >>180–1, 184

Two pairs of figures carved from laurel wood, considered sacred and known as *chemamules*, depict an old and young couple that represent wisdom and the continuity of life. Out front stands an iron and *raulí* sculpture inspired by a Holy Stone, used traditionally to give thanks for the harvest with wine and chicken blood. Almaviva's logo, a Mapuche emblem representing the cosmos, is featured in natural pigments on the barrel cellar's end screen.

So where's the French in all of this? According to Hurtado, it's in the "elegance and attention to detail". A series of lateral metal slats on the exterior add a vibrantly modern feel, and act as a discreet counterpoint to the curves of the roof. The barrel cellar is modelled on that of Mouton-Rothschild, the visual effect enhanced by a floor and roof designed to converge. On the wine's label, next to the Mapuche logo, the word "Almaviva" is an exact copy of French author Beaumarchais' original handwriting (the name is taken from his great work *The Marriage of Figaro*).

Almaviva is a combination of French experience, Chilean grapes and a whole mish-mash of cross-cultural sparks in between. In the winery, Martín Hurtado has brought this background to life in vivid, imaginative fashion. "It speaks for itself," he remarks, "when you come and get to know it."

I think it's appropriate to end in Chile, whose people refer to it as the end of the earth, and at a winery that is nothing more than a winery, as simple as it is evocative. We started at the heart of the Old World at Bordeaux's Château Margaux and we end at the dawn of a New World in the Maipo Valley, a short distance from Almaviva.

If Almaviva was a watershed for Chile, then Pérez Cruz is a worthy, if independently minded, successor. The winery was built by José Cruz Ovalle, another Iberian name to add to the long and distinguished list of Spanish architects to have graced the world of wine. The Pérez Cruz family, owners of

Pérez Cruz CHILE ≫184, 186–7

a large estate outside Santiago, were looking to build a winery and make a name for themselves in the wine business. They ran a small competition; Cruz won.

Cruz was not an unknown quantity in Chile, however. He had worked on the stunning Hotel Explora in Patagonia with Germán del Sol, who built the Gracia winery (see p.126). The Explora was a landmark for Chilean tourism, ruinously expensive for the average Chilean, but utter luxury inside a warm wood structure, with unimpeded views over breathtaking Antarctic scenery. It took advantage of its surroundings to create a simple but dramatic effect. It also managed to be distinctly Chilean.

In Pérez Cruz, the architect had a very different location and function to contend with. In choosing to work with simple materials and shapes, Cruz avoided any expansive gestures, but in the winery's simplicity has created a remarkably powerful piece of architecture. The upturned cup-and-saucer design essentially consists of two barrel vaults side by side, topped by a jointed roof.

Although stone and metal do feature, the overriding impression is of pure wood, especially in the graceful curves of the exterior roof supports.

It's a carefully contrived effect, and a very Chilean one at that, with strong, flexible wooden lines framed by sharp sunlight. Inside, the effect is magnified with clever use of skylights and windows to filter light and air throughout the wooden structure. A cavity between the roof and two vaults channels this light and air, also making for an atmospheric gallery. The architecture seems full of natural energy.

What's strange about Almaviva and Pérez Cruz is that the more you contemplate them, the less they seem "modern". The wood, the simple designs, the lack of pretensions to grandeur – this is all basic stuff. And yet, in their own way, these two wineries are just as affecting and innovative as the work of Calatrava and Gehry, or Eiffel and Palladio in their day. They have all served wine nobly. Any preference is a simple matter of taste.

IN BRIEF

YSIOS
Rioja, Spain
BUILT 2001 by Santiago Calatrava
WINE TIP Vendimia Seleccionada
VISITS By appointment
www.byb.es

Just one of many wine estates owned by giant Spanish group Bodegas y Bebidas, Ysios is not about to get lost in the crowd. Calatrava's astonishing buildings fuse engineering and sculpture to create elegant drama. The wines are finding their way towards the eventual aim of lovingly crafted, single-estate Riojan reds.

MARQUES DE RISCAL
Rioja, Spain
COMPLETION 2005 by Frank Gehry
WINE TIP Barón de Chirel
VISITS By appointment
www.marquesderiscal.com

One of Rioja's oldest and finest wineries, Riscal has often been its boldest pioneer. Groundbreaking wines such as Barón de Chirel have set the scene for Riscal's modern renaissance. Now architect Frank Gehry is set to stun the dusty, warm-stone town of Elciego with space-age architecture. Old boys in berets, watch out.

LE CLOS JORDANNE
Niagara Peninsula, Ontario, Canada
COMPLETION 2007 by Frank Gehry

The region is Niagara Peninsula, the grapes Chardonnay and Pinot Noir. The combination is due to some joint-venturing between Canada's Vincor and Burgundy's Boisset – one country's land, another region's grapes, and the world's most famous architect for good measure. Gehry is on record as promising the creation of "a cathedral for wine".

IRIUS
Somontano, Spain
COMPLETION 2005 by Jesús Marino Pascual
VISITS Open doors
www.grupoproconsol.com

A blank canvas in the form of Somontano's bleak landscape affords plenty of creative opportunities for modern styles of wine, as well as architecture. Not content with simply being a birthplace for modern wine, Irius sets out to be a landmark in its own right. It's one architect's vision of the future of wine.

ANTION
Rioja, Spain
COMPLETION 2005 by Jesús Marino Pascual
VISITS Open doors
www.grupoproconsol.com

Same architect as Irius (above), same owners, very different result. Set in the eye of Rioja's architectural storm, near Ysios and Riscal, Antion's architect had a tricky job designing the winery and hotel around an odd-shaped plot of land. It carries the fight to its eminent neighbours.

DARIEN
Rioja, Spain
BUILT 2004 by Jesús Marino Pascual
WINE TIP Darien Crianza
VISITS Open doors
www.darien.es

Rioja is alive with the clamour of new wine architecture, and projects like Darien show why. Everyone wants a piece of the action. Set by the roadside between some of the region's most traditional producers, both Darien's architecture and wine are fresh and modern, but feel very local.

Pérez Cruz SPAIN

Antion SPAIN

Darien SPAIN

WINERIES WITH STYLE

DOMINUS
Napa Valley, USA
BUILT 1997 by Herzog & de Meuron
WINE TIP Dominus 1994
VISITS Trade only
www.dominusestate.com

Aloof and elusive, Dominus is related by ownership to Bordeaux superstar Château Pétrus. Its wines, essentially Bordeaux blends, are just as ambitious – the idea is to work as closely with nature as possible. The results are refreshingly elegant wines for Napa, though highly priced. The winery is unique; too bad it's closed to the public.

DISZNOKO
Tokaji, Hungary
BUILT 1995 by Dezsö Ekler
WINE TIP Tokaji Aszú 6 puttonyos
VISITS Open doors
www.disznoko.hu

Great to see a Hungarian winery (albeit French owned) setting the standard for wine design. When AXA took over in 1992, Hungary was emerging giddy from communist rule. Now Disznókő is making Tokaji in a firmly modern style – still luxuriant, rich, and sweet, but with less oxidation and more fruit than before.

VERGELEGEN
Helderberg, Stellenbosch, South Africa
BUILT 1992 by Dillon and de Gastines
WINE TIP Vergelegen White
VISITS Open doors
www.vergelegen.co.za

Some of South Africa's very best wines emerge from this property, owned by mining group Anglo-American Corporation. The location is the key – overlooking False Bay, with its fresh breezes and temperate climate. A striking hilltop winery pays homage to this landscape, as well as the estate's history that stretches back to 1700.

MEZZACORONA
Trentino, Italy
BUILT 1997 onwards by Alberto Cecchetto
WINE TIP Teroldego Rotaliano Riserva
VISITS Open doors
www.mezzacorona.it

Huge cooperative wineries aren't always known for their forward thinking, so it's cheering to see Mezzacorona making a splash with its vibrant architecture. In this mountainous part of Italy, stony cliff faces, steep pergola vines and fractious land ownership are the norms – Mezzacorona absorbs and expresses these influences admirably.

ALMAVIVA
Puente Alto, Maipo, Chile
BUILT 1999 by Martín Hurtado
WINE TIP Almaviva 2000
VISITS By appointment
www.conchaytoro.com

Almaviva is a French-Chilean joint-venture, a bit like fusion cooking, with a French chef and Chilean ingredients. The one wine made here is a Bordeaux blend, though with the addition of former Bordeaux variety (and now Chilean specialty) Carmenère. Wine and winery aim for iconic status; both manage to incorporate an earthy Chilean feel. Stunning.

PEREZ CRUZ
Maipo, Chile
BUILT 2002 by José Cruz Ovalle
WINE TIP Reserva Limited Edition Cot
VISITS By appointment
www.perezcruz.com

Chile's success of late has spelled boom. Those who were simply grape growers now want their name on a bottle. New wineries spring up – some tedious, others inspiring. Some, like Pérez Cruz, stake their name in vivid architectural language. How can such simple ingredients (wood, light) create such exhilarating spaces?

Marqués de Riscal SPAIN

Almaviva CHILE

Vergelegen SOUTH AFRICA

A NEW WORLD 189

BIBLIOGRAPHY

This book was so enjoyable to research that I became a bit like the proverbial kid in a sweet shop. The range and number of sources I have consulted means that this bibliography is far from exhaustive. There just isn't enough space to provide a more comprehensive list of books and, especially, the many fascinating articles in periodicals I shuffled through in the library at the Royal Institute of British Architects.

Though it is a small gesture, I would like to thank and acknowledge all those who have brought architecture and wine to life and, ultimately, helped craft this book.

Alberto Cecchetto, *Paesaggio in Bottiglia*, Le Nuove Cantine Rotari e MezzaCorona, Verona, Cierre Edizione and Grupo Mezzacorona, 1997
Jean Dethier ed., *Chateaux Bordeaux*, London, Mitchell Beazley, 1989
Susan Doubilet, *Wine in a Manger*, Progressive Architecture Volume 66 number April 4 ,1985 p98
Gustave Eiffel, *L'Architecture Metallique*, Paris, Maisonneuve et Larose, 1996
Nicholas Faith, *Château Margaux*, Christie's Wine Publishing, London, 1980
Sir Bannister Fletcher, A History of Architecture on the Comparative Method, B.T. Batsford, Ltd., London, 1921
Mildred Friedman ed. and Michael Sorkin, *Gehry Talks, Architecture + Process*, London, Thames & Hudson, 2003
Carl I. Gable, (lecture adapted under the title) *The Secrets of Palladio's Villas*, www.boglewood.com
Jonathan Glancey, *The Story of Architecture*, Dorling Kindersley, London, 2000
Andrew Jefford, *The New France, A Complete Guide to Contemporary French Wine*, Mitchell Beazley, London, 2002
Charles Jencks ed., *Frank O Gehry, Individual Imagination and Cultural Conservatism*. London. Academy Editions, 1995

Hugh Johnson and Jancis Robinson, *The World Atlas of Wine*, 5th Edition, Mitchell Beazley, London, 2001
Hugh Johnson's Story of Wine, Mitchell Beazley, London, 1989
Jean-Pierre Méric, *Le Château d'Arsac de 1706 à Nos Jours*, Editions Féret, Bordeaux, 2000
Dirk Meyhöfer, *The Architecture of Wine, Building Art and Wine Growing in Bordeaux and the Napa Valley*, photography by Olaf Gollnek. Ludwigsburg. AVedition, 1999
Andrea Palladio, *I Quattro Libri dell'Architettura*, English (*The Four Books of Architecture*), translated by Robert Tavernor and Richard Schofield, Cambridge, Mass., London, MIT, 1997
Rod Phillips, *A Short History of Wine*, Allen Lane, The Penguin Press, 2000
Prince Alain de Polignac, *Madame Pommery, Le Genie et le Coeur*, Stock, 1994
Prince Alain de Polignac, (lecture entitled) *Une Architecture Au Service d'une Marque*, delivered in Reims on November 7, 1998
John Radford, *The New Spain, A Complete Guide to Contemporary Spanish Wine*, Mitchell Beazley, London, 1998
John Ruskin, *The Seven Lamps of Architecture*, London, Smith, Elder & Co., 1849
Schleicher, Seeliber and Staab, Schloss Johannisberg, *Nine Centuries of Wine and Culture on the Rhine*, Woschek-Verlag, Mainz
Keith Stewart, *Te Mata, The First 100 Years*, Godwit, Auckland, 1997
Chateau Tahbilk, *The First 135 Years*, 4th Edition, Tahbilk Proprietary Ltd., Melbourne, 1995
Hanno-Walter Kruft, *Geschichte der Architekturtheorie*, English (*A History of Architectural Theory, from Vitruvius to the Present*), translated by Ronald Taylor, Elsie Callander and Anthony Wood, London, Zwemmer, 1994
Piero Zoi, *Cantina del Redi, Vecchia Cantian di Montepulciano SCARL*, Siena, 2002

INDEX
Page numbers in **bold** refer to principal text for winery; those in ***bold italic*** refer to factboxes; those in *italic* refer to illustrations.

Abbazia de Novacella 27, **31**, *39*
Abram *128*
Acosta, Alejandro d' *161*
Adel, Elena 57, 59
Airò, Mario 100
Alcorta, Juan **57**, *59*, *60*, *61*, *67*, ***67***
Allen, Max 95
Almaviva 4, **180–1**, *184*, **184**, *189*, ***189***
Alois Lageder Löwengang 98, **100–2**, *101*, *102*, *128*, ***129***
Antion **169**, *173*, *188*, ***188***
architects 22
　Abram (Löwengang) *128*
　Acosta (Santo Tomás) *161*
　Arnaudo (Terre da Vino) *160*
　Athfield (Te Mata) 95, *97*
　Beerstecher (Rustenberg) 88, 90, *97*
　Blair (Craggy Range) 138, *160*
　Bo (Ca' Marcanda) 110, *111*, *128*
　Bofill (Lafite-Rothschild) 51, *66*, 75
　Bórmida (Salentein; Séptima) 60, *67*, *106*, *128*
　Bouligny (Artesa) *67*
　Boyd (Mitchelton) *97*
　Burghardt (Loimer) *96*
　Burgos (Haras de Pirque) *161*
　Cabinet Arc (Viret Clos du Paradis) *128*
　Cabinet Cohérence (Haut Selve) *160*
　Cabinet Seturec (La Sablière) *160*
　Calatrava (Ysios) 166, *167*, *188*
　Cecchetto (Mezzacorona) 177, *178*, **180**, ***189***
　Combe (Margaux) 20, *38*
Cruz Ovalle (Pérez Cruz) 184, 186, *189*
Dillon (Pichon-Longueville; Vergelegen) 75, *96*, 174, *189*
Doriga (Domecq La Mezquita) *66*
Dubuisson (Haut Selve) 142
Eiffel (González Byass) 50, *66*
Ekler (Disznókő) 174, *189*
Elias (Catena Zapata) *129*
Gastines (Pichon-Longueville; Vergelegen) 75, *96*, 174, *189*
Gehry (Jordanne; Riscal) 133, 167, 168, ***188***
Gosset (Pommery) *66*
Gozier (Pommery) *66*
Graves (Pegase) 75, *96*
Grenon (Coltibuono) 82, *96*
Hadid (López de Heredia) 87, *97*
Hennemann (Romanin) 104, *128*
Hernandez (Arsac) 79, *96*
Herzog (Dominus) 171, *189*
Hurtado (Almaviva) 181, *189*
Johnson, Scott (Opus One) 118, 120
Johnson Fain Partners (Opus One) *129*
Jordi (Hess) *96*
Kundig, Tom (Mission Hill) 114
Malherbe (Dornier) 143, *160*
Marino Pascual (Antion; Darien; Irius) 169, *170*, *171*, ***188***
Marsh (Shadowfax) *129*
Mattes (Weinsberg) *160*
Mazières (Viña Real) *160*
Meuron (Dominus) 171, *189*
Moneo (Arínzano) 81, *96*
Neumann (Hofkeller) *39*
Olsen Sundberg Kundig Allen (Mission Hill) *128*
Palladio (Maser) 22, *38*
Paterson (Sileni) 148, *161*
Peruzzi (Redi) 48, *66*
Prandtauer (FWW) 34, *39*
Propst (Malivoire) *161*
Puig i Cadafalch (Codorníu) 52, *67*
Quemada (Alcorta) 57, *67*
Rehm (Sileni) *161*
Rubió i Bellver (Raimat) 52, *67*
Sartogo (Coltibuono) 82, *96*
Schnabl (Löwengang) *128*
Scott (Ransom) 140, *160*
Sol (Gracia) 126, *127*, *129*
Strauch-Stoll (Wackerbarth) *96*
Torroja Cavanillas (González Byass) 50, *66*
Triay (Artesa; Raimat) 51–2, 53, *67*
UKZ (Wiemer) *97*
Volgyesi (Malivoire) 156, *161*
Walker (Waterford) 114, *128*
Wessels (Coastal Cellar) 145, *161*
Woodfall (Rymill) 148, *161*
Yanzón (Salentein; Séptima) 60, *67*, *106*, *107*, *128*
Yianniotis (Santorini) *129*
architectural competitions 71, 75, 186
architecture 17, 86, 140
　wineries 22, 34, 75, 85
Argentina 59, 106, 121
Arínzano, Chivite Señorío de 80, **81–2**, *96*, *97*
Arnaudo, Gianni *160*
Arnold, Kevin 114
Arsac, Château d' 76, 77, *77*, **79–80**, *96*, ***96***
Artesa **53**, *57*, *58*, *59*, ***67***
Athfield, John 95, *97*
Ausone, Château 46, 47, *47*, **47–8**, *66*, ***66***
Australia 90, 95, 148
Austria 34
AXA 174
AXA-Millésimes 77

Baden 144
Badenhorst, Adi 88, 90
Badia a Coltibuono *81*, **82**, *96*
Barbaro, Villa *see* Villa di Maser
Barbaro brothers 22
Barlow, Simon 88
Barolo 139
Barré, Vincent 142
Bauhaus 143
Bavaria 34–5
Beerstecher, Simon 88, 90, *97*
Bekaa Valley 24
Bilbao 165, 166
biodynamics 103–4
Blair, John 138, *160*
Bo, Giovanni 110, *111*, *128*
bodegas 46
Bofill, Ricardo 51, *66*, 75
Boisset 168
Bonneau du Martray 140
Bordeaux 20, 22, 36, 48, 51, 75, 76–7, 141, 142

190　WINERIES WITH STYLE

Bordes, Juan 142
Bórmida, Eliana 60, *67*, 106, **128**
Bouligny *67*
Boulton, Roger 170–1
Boutari Santorini *122*, *123*, **125–6**, *128*, **129**
Boyd, Robin *97*
British Columbia 114
Brixen, Bishop of 31
Buck, John and Wendy 95
Burghardt, Andreas *96*
Burgos, Jaime *161*
Burgundy 138, 140, 168

Ca' Marcanda **107**, *109*, **110–11**, **128**
Cabinet Arc **128**
Cabinet Cohérence **160**
Cabinet Seturec **160**
Cadafalch *see* Puig i Cadafalch
Calatrava, Santiago 165, 166, 167, 169, **188**
California 61, 75
Campania 48
Canada 102, 114, 155, 168
Cape Dutch 87–8, 177
Carlos, Juan 138
Castan, Vianney 47
Castel Noarna 20, 24, *27*, **38**
Catalonia 52, 53
Catena, Nicolás 121, 122
Catena Zapata *117*, *118*, **121–3**, **128**, **129**
cava 52, 53
Caves Rocbère 47
Cecchetto, Alberto 177, 178, 180, **189**
Champagne 47
Champy, Boris 174
château 24, 36
Château d'Arsac *76*, *77*, **77**, *79–80*, *96*, **96**
Château Ausone *46*, 47, *47*, **47–8**, *66*, **66**
Château Haut Selve *141*, **141–2**, **160**
Château Ksara 20, *21*, 24, **38**, *39*
Château Lafite-Rothschild **51**, *53*, *66*, 75, 138
Château Margaux 14, **16**, **20**, **22**, 34, 36, **38**, **39**, 88
Château Pétrus 171
Château Pichon-Longueville Baron 72, *73*, *74*, *75*, **75–6**, 77, *96*, 174
Château Romanin **102–4**, *104*, **128**
Château des Rontets 140
Châteaux Bordeaux Exhibition 75
Chianti 82
Chile 159, 180
Chivite Señorío de Arínzano 80, **81–2**, **96**, **97**
Christöphler, Jörg 85, 86
Cipes, Stephen 102
Cistercians 31
Cittadella del Vino, La 178
Clos Jordanne, Le **167–8**, *169*, **188**
Clos Pegase 9, 68, *70*, **71**, *75*, *96*, **96**
Coastal Cellar, Graham Beck *7*, **145**, *147*, *148*, **148**, *149*, **161**
Codorníu **52–3**, *56*, *57*, *67*, **67**, 106, 107
Coltibuono, Badia a *81*, *82*, **96**
Combe, Louis 20, **38**
competitions, architectural *71*, 75, 186
computer-aided design 169
Concha, La 50
Concha y Toro 180
Coonawarra 148
cooperatives 139, 177
Copas, Las 50

Corbières 47
Cos d'Estournel *6*, 36, **36**, *37*, *39*, **39**
Cosío, Santiago 155
cosmoculture 105
Craggy Range *136*, *137*, **138**, *160*
Crimea 35
Cruz Ovalle, José 184, *186*, **189**
CVNE 132
Cyclades 125

Daedalus 42
Darien 169, **170**, *174*, *188*, **188**
Dethier, Jean 75
Dillon, Patrick 75, *96*, 174, **189**
Disznókő *9*, *174*, *178*, *179*, **189**
Domaine Huët 103
Domaine Viret Clos du Paradis *105*, **105**, **128**
Domecq La Mezquita *40*, *46*, *66*
Dominus *171*, *174*, *175*, *176*, *177*, **189**
Doriga, Javier Soto López *66*
Dornier **142–3**, *143*, **160**
Dornier, Christoph 143
Doubilet, Susan 87
Dubuisson, Sylvain 142

Eiffel, Gustave 50, *66*, 132
Eiffel Tower 132
Ekler, Dezsö 174, **189**
Elias, Pablo Sánchez **129**
Estournel, Cos d' *6*, 36, **36**, *37*, *39*, **39**
evolution 31
Eymael, Jean 31
Eymael, Robert 31

Fitou 47
Freie Weingärtner Wachau (FWW) *29*, 30, 34, **39**

Gable, Carl I: 22
Gaja, Angelo 107
Galante, Pepe 122
García Sedano, Juan Carlos 132
Gastines, Jean de 75, *96*, 174, **189**
Gaudí, Antoni 52, 86
Gazeau-Montrasi, Fabio 140
Gehry, Frank 133, 166, 167, 168, 169, **188**
Germany 27, 31, 34–5, 143
Gertsch, Franz 80
Giants Winery 138
Glancey, Jonathan 17, 122
González Byass 48, *50*, *52*, *66*
Gosset *66*
Goulburn River 90, 95
Gozier *66*
Gracia **126–7**, *127*, **129**
Graham Beck Coastal Cellar *7*, **145**, *147*, *148*, **148**, *149*, **161**
Graves 141
Graves, Michael 75, *96*
gravity-concept wineries 153–4, 156, 159
Greece 125
Greiffenclau, Erwein 27
Greiffenclau, Karl-Philipp von 35
Greiffenclau family 27
Grenon, Nathalie 82, *96*

Hadid, Zaha 87, *97*
Haras de Pirque *159*, *158*, *159*, *161*, **161**
Haut Selve, Château *141*, **141–2**, **160**
Hawke's Bay 95, 138, 148
Hennemann, Serge 104, **128**
Hermann J Wiemer *86*, 87, *87*, *97*
Hernandez, Patrick 79, *96*
Herzog 171, **189**

Hess Collection 78, 79, 80, *96*, **96**
Hess, Donald 80
Heverin, Jim 87
history 24, 31
Hofkeller Würzburg, Staatlicher 31, *33*, **35**, **38**, **39**
holistic approach 101–2
Huët, Domaine 103
Hungary 174
Hurtado, Martin 181, **189**

Irius 169, *171*, **188**
Italy 22, 24, 31, 48, 100, 107, 139, 177

Jarvis 61, *64*, 65, **65**, *67*
Johannisberg, Schloss 24, 25, *27*, **38**
Johner, Irene 16
Johner, Karl 16
Johner winery 16
Johnson, Hugh 27, 35, 48, 144
Johnson, Scott 118, 120
Johnson Fain Partners **129**
Jordanne, Le Clos **167–8**, *169*, **188**
Jordi, Beat *96*
Juan Alcorta 57, *59*, 60, 61, *67*, **67**

Kellerschlössel 34
Ksara, Château 20, *21*, 24, **38**, *39*
Kundig, Tom 114

La Sablière, Louis Jadot **135**, *136*, **138**, *160*, **160**
Lafite-Rothschild, Château **51**, *53*, *66*, 75, 138
Lageder, Alois 100–2
Lardière, Jacques 133, 136, 138
Lázaro, José Luis 169
Le Bault de la Morinière, Jean-Charles 140
Lebanon 24
Leda group 141
Lesgourgues, Jean-Jacques 141
Loimer 82, **83**, *96*
Loimer, Fred 83
López de Heredia 84, 85, **86–7**, *97*, **97**
López de Heredia, María 86
Louis Jadot La Sablière **135**, *136*, **138**, *160*, **160**
Löwengang, Alois Lageder *98*, **100–2**, *101*, *102*, **128**, **129**

Malherbe, Johan 143, **160**
Malivoire **155–6**, *156*, *157*, **161**, *161*
Malivoire, Martin 155
Mandl, Anthony von 114
Margaux, Château 14, **16**, **20**, **22**, 34, 36, **38**, **39**, 88
Marino Pascual, Jesús *9*, 169, *170*, 171, **188**
Marlborough 138
Marqués de Riscal 166, *167*, **167**, 168, **188**, *189*
Marsh, Wood **129**
Martinborough 138
Maser, Villa di 17, *19*, **22**, **38**, *38*
Massandra 34, 35, **35–6**, *39*
Mastroberardino 48, *49*, *50*, *51*, *66*
Mastroberardino, Antonio 48
Mastroberardino, Piero 48
Matabos, Bernard 141, 142
Matignon, Jean-René 76
Matte, Eduardo 159
Mattes, Hugo **160**
Maya 122
Mazières, Philippe 132, **160**
Meinert, Martin 177
Mendoza 106, 121
Metternich, Tatiana Princess von 27
Meuron, de 171, **189**
Mexico 152

Mezzacornona **177–8**, **180**, *181*, *182*, **189**
Mies van der Rohe 140, 143
Mission Hill 111, 113, **114**, **128**
Mitchelton 90, 93, **95**, **97**
monasteries 31
Mönchhof 26, **31**, *39*
Mondavi, Robert 118, 121
Moneo, Rafael 81, *96*
Montepulciano 48
Mosel Valley 31
Moueix, Christian 171
Müller, Christian Philipp 102
Mykonos 125

Napa Valley 80, 114, 123
Naudé, Ian 142, 143
Neumann, Balthasar *39*
New World 151–2
New York State 87
New Zealand 95, 138, 140, 148, 151
Newton, Peter 123
Niagara Peninsula 168
Nicholas II: 35
Noarna, Castel 20, 24, *27*, **38**
Novacella, Abbazia de 27, **31**, *39*

Olsen Sundberg Kundig Allen **128**
Ontario 155
Opus One 114, **114**, 115, 118, **120–1**, **129**
ownership, change of 31

Palladio, Andrea 22, **38**, 42
Paterson, Dodd *161*
Paterson, George 148
Pegase, Clos 9, 68, *70*, **70**, **71**, *75*, *96*, **96**
Pérez Cruz *9*, *184*, 185, **186–7**, *187*, *188*, **189**
Pérez Cruz family 184
Peruzzi, Baldassare 48, *66*
Pétrus, Château 171
Pichon-Longueville Baron, Château 72, *73*, *74*, *75*, **75–6**, 77, *96*, 174
Piedmont 139
Pinguet, Noël 103
Pommery 42, *43*, *44*, *47*, *66*, **66**
Pommery, Madame 47
Pompeii 48
Pontallier, Paul 20
Prandtauer, Jakob 34, *39*
Proconsol 169
Propst *161*
Provence 103
Puig i Cadafalch, Josep 52, *67*
Purbick, Alister 95
pyramids 102, 122

Quemada, Ignacio 57, *67*

Radford, John 53
Raimat **52**, *55*, *66*, *67*
Ransom 140, **140–1**, *160*
Ransom, Robin 140, 141
Raventós, Manuel 52
Raventós, Ricard 107
Raventós family 52
Real, Viña 130, 132, **132–3**, 133, **160**, *160*
Redi 48, **48**, *66*
Rehm, Bukowski *161*
religion 24, 31
religious communities 31
Rheingau 27
Rioja 57, 86, 132, 133, 166, 170
Riscal, Marqués de 166, *167*, **167**, 168, **188**, 189
Robinson, Jancis 35, 144

INDEX 191

Rocbère, Caves 47
Romanin, Château **102–4**, 104, *128*
Rontets, Château des 140
Rothschild, Eric de 51, 138
Rothschild family (Château Mouton-Rothschild) 118, 121, 180
Rubió i Bellver 52, *67*
Ruskin, John 27, 163
Rustenberg 88, **88**, 89, 90, **90**, 97, *97*
Rymill **148**, 150, 151, 161, *161*
Rymill, Peter 148

Salentein 59–60, 63, 67, *67*, 106
Santo Tomás **152–3**, 154, 155, **155**, *161*
Santorini 125
Santorini, Boutari 122, 123, **125–6**, 128, *129*
Sartogo, Piero 82, *96*
Schloss Johannisberg 24, 25, *27*, *38*
Schloss Vollrads 22, 23, *27*, 38, *38*
Schloss Wackerbarth 83, **85–6**, *96*
Schnabl 128
Schwegler, Martin 143, 145
Scott, Graeme 140, *160*
Séptima 106, **106–7**, 107, *128*

Shadowfax 124, 125, 126, **126**, 129, *129*
sherry 46, 48
Shrem, Jan 70
Sileni **148**, **151**, 152, 153, *161*
Smith, Steve 138
Sol, Germán del 126, 127, **129**, 186
South Africa 113, 142, 145
Spain 46, 52, 81, 165
sparkling wine 53
Sperling, Ann 156
St-Emilion 48
Staatlicher Hofkeller Würzburg 31, 33, **35**, 38, *39*
Staatsweingut Weinsberg **143–5**, 144, 145, *160*
Stellenbosch 88
Sterling 119, 120, 121, **123–5**, *129*
Strauch-Stoll, Thomas *96*
Summerhill **102–3**, 103, *128*, 129

Tahbilk 90, 91, 92, **95**, *97*
Tchelistcheff, Dmitri 65
Te Mata 94, 95, **95**, *97*
Teipolo, Giovanni Battista 35
Terra-Vinéa 45, **47**, *66*
Terre da Vino 138, **138–40**, 139, 160, *160*

terroir 138
Tokaji 174
Torrengo, Cristina 140
Torroja Cavanillas, J A 50, *66*
Trafford, David 148
Trentino 24, 177
Triay, Domingo 51–2, 53, *67*
Tuscany 107

U
underground places 24
USA 114

Vauthier, Alain 48
Vergelegen 75, **174**, **177**, 180, 189, *189*
Versailles 34
Victoria, Australia 90
Villa Barbaro *see* Villa di Maser
Villa di Maser 17, 19, **22**, 38, *38*
Viña Gracia *see* Gracia
Viña Real 130, 132, **132–3**, 133, 160, *160*
Vincor 168
Viret, Alain 105
Viret, Philippe 105
Viret Clos du Paradis, Domaine 105, *105*, *128*

Vitruvius 17
Volgyesi, Andrew 156, *161*
Vollrads, Schloss 22, 23, *27*, 38, *38*
Voyatzis, Yannis 125

Wachau 34
Wackerbarth, Schloss 83, **85–6**, *96*
Walker, Alex 114, *128*
Waterford 110, **113–14**, *128*, *128*
Weinsberg, Staatsweingut **143–5**, 144, 145, *160*
Wessels, Johan 145, *161*
Wiemer, Hermann J 86, 87, **87**, *97*
wine cellars 31, **40–65**
wine schools 143
wineries 36, 80
 architecture 22, 34, 75, 85
Woodfall, Geoffrey 148, *161*
Wright, Frank Lloyd 143
Württemberg 144

Yanzón, Mario 60, *67*, 106, 107, *128*
Yianniotis, Yiannis *129*
Ysios 162, 164, 165, **166–7**, *188*

Zoi, Piero 48

ACKNOWLEDGEMENTS

My sincere thanks go out to the following people.

To the team at Mitchell Beazley, the firm foundations for this book: I could not have worked with a more professional, talented and likeable group of people. Thank you to Hilary Lumsden, Yasia Williams, Tim Pattinson, and Juanne Branquinho as well as Susan Low for her patient and intelligent editing.

To the wineries themselves, as well as their architects, for giving generously of their time, help and hospitality. Oh, and for building some inspirational wineries in the first place.

To all those many people, lovers of wine and architecture, whose help has been like hundreds of steady pillars of support for the project. Specifically, I would like to thank Max Allen, Lynn Alley, Ulrike Bahm, Sally Bishop, Roger Boulton, Céline Bouteiller, Michael Broadbent, Stephen Brook, Bob Campbell, Sabine Cleizergues, Clemence de Crécy, Nick Faith, Akos Forczek, Rosemary George, Susannah George, Tom Gilbey, Emma Little, Catherine Manac'h, Marcelo Marasco, Jo Mason, André Morgenthal, Françoise Peretti, Tom Perry, Florence Raffard, Jen Ramage, Phil Reedman, Sophie Waggett and Jeremy Watson.

Lastly, thanks to Anne-Claude Leflaive for her characteristically astute and questioning reception – for she is the nameless producer in the introduction. To my agent, Barbara Levy. And to my family, whose opinion and company I always cherish. Finally, to Susie, to whom no thanks could ever be enough.

Any remaining mistakes are my responsibility. Equally, if you know of any worthy wineries that have not been included, please let me know at pete@devinitywine.com (no attachments, please).

Mitchell Beazley would like to thank the following for their kind permission to reproduce the photographs in this book.

t top, m middle, b bottom, l left, r right

Jacket picture Arcaid Picture Library

Peter Richards
4–5, 14, 12 row 2 pic 4 & 16, 23, 25, 26, 38 m, 38 b, 60, 61 t, 12 row 4 pic 1 & 64, 13 row 1 pic 3 & 68, 70–1, 77, 78, 80 t, 96 m, 96 b, 97 m, 110t, 110 b, 120 t, 13 row 1 pic 1 & 121, 128 m, 129 t, 134–5, 144, 146–7, 148–9, 154–155, 160 m, 180 t, 189 m

Courtesy of wineries
6, 7, 9 t, 9 m, 9 b, 12 row 4 pic 3 & 17–19, 20 t, 20 b r, 20 b l, 12 row 1 pic 2 & 22, (12 row 2 pic 3 & 21, 24, 27, 12 row 1 pic & 28-30, 31–33, 12 row 2 pic 1 & 36-37, 38 t, 39 t, 39 m, 39 b, 42– 44, 12 row 3 pic 3 & 45, 48, 12 row 5 pic 1 & 13 row 2 pic 4 & 49–51, 52, 13 row 4 pic 3 & 53, 13 row 2 pic 3 & 13 row 5 pic 1 & 54–55, 56–57, 13 row 3 pic 2 & 13 row 5 pic 3 & 58–59, 61 m, 61 b, 13 row 4 pic 4 & 62–63, 65, 66 t, 66 m, 67 t, 67 m, 67 b, 12 row 5 pic 2 & 13 row 3 pic 3 & 72–75, 12 row 4 pic 4 & 76, 12 row 5 pic 3 & 79, 13 row 3 pic 4 & 80 b & 97 b, 81, 82–83 t, 83 b, 86–87, 93, 94–95, 96 t, 13 row 5 pic 2 & 13 row 5 pic 4 & 98–102, 103, 104 l, 13 row 2 pic 2 & 104 r–105, 106–107, 13 row 1 pic 2 & 108–109, 12 row 5 pic 4 & 111–113, 13 row 2 pic 1 & 114–115, 12 row 4 pic 2 & 116–118, 119, 120 b, 122–123, 12 row 1 pic 4 & 124–126, 13 row 4 pic 2 & 127, 128, 129m, 129 b, 136–137, 138–139, 141, 142–143, 145, 150–151, 152–153, 154–155, 158–161 m, 160 t, 161 b, 162–165, 166–168 & 189 t, 175–177, 178–179, 12 row 2 pic 2 & 180 b –181 & 189 b, 182–183, 184, 185–187 & 188 t

Photographers / Organizations
34–35 Phil Baker at blacksea-crimea.com – Massandra; 13 row 4 pic 2 & 40 Rocio Benitez Fiol – La Mezquita, Domecq; 12 row 1 pic 1 & 12 row 3 pic 2 & 46–47 & 66 b © Serge Bois-Prevost – Château Ausone; 12 row 3 pic 1 & 13 row 1 pic 4 & 84–85 © Jesus Rocandio/Camara Oscura – Lopez De Heredia; 88–90 & 97 t Graphic Shop, Design & Branding Agency – Rustenberg; 12 row 3 pic 4 & 13 row 3 pic 1 & 91–92 Kieth Lucas Design Pty Ltd – Tahbilk; 130–133, 160 b © Fotomàs – Viña Real; 140 Michael Ng – Randsom; 156–157, 161 t © Steven Elpuick at Velocite – Malivoire; 169 Frank Gehry & Associates Inc – Le Clos Jordanne; 170–174 & 188m & 188 b – Vinédos y Bodegas XXI / Darien

WINERIES WITH STYLE